FOOTBALL IN A PANDEMIC

SAM HUDSON

FOOTBALL IN A PANDEMIC

AN INSIGHT INTO THE STRATEGIES AND TACTICS USED DURING THE 2020/21 PREMIER LEAGUE SEASON

First published by Pitch Publishing, 2021

Pitch Publishing
A2 Yeoman Gate
Yeoman Way
Worthing
Sussex
BN13 3QZ
www.pitchpublishing.co.uk
info@pitchpublishing.co.uk

A CIP catalogue record is available for this book
from the British Library.

ISBN: 978 1 78531 991 4

Typesetting and origination by Pitch Publishing
Printed and bound in India by Replika Press Pvt. Ltd.

Contents

Acknowledgements

THIS PROJECT has stemmed from a lifelong passion for the game, how it's played, and the intricacies, ideas, and extremely talented individuals who fill various roles. My own coaching career began back in 2011, and I am extremely grateful for the advice, assistance, and, more than anything, time given to me by Mark Neville, Dave Adams, Dave Gough, and Dick Bate, especially during my university years. They gave me the best platform into the world of football anyone could wish for, and truly lit the fire within to forge a career in the game.

Kevin Metcalfe, Tom Skeath, and Daf Williams, who I also met via university, have also furthered my knowledge over the years. Whether that's through the most casual of discussions within a bar, or through lengthy calls and FaceTimes, these three have not only proved to be extremely talented and knowledgeable in their own respective environments and clubs, but also three individuals I cannot speak highly enough of.

Glen Buckley is also indirectly responsible for my passion towards the game, as an extremely experienced, knowledgeable, and funny man. My time working abroad is full of fond memories both on and off the field, yet it is no exaggeration that Glen has been one of the most influential individuals within my career. His ability to take the most complex and difficult ideas, and simplify them without losing any of the detail, is a skill I'll never forget, and hopefully something I can one day replicate to his standard.

Jon Woodward has also proven to be another fantastic mentor, coach, educator, and good friend who has always made time in his busy schedule for me. Whether that's critiquing my on-field delivery, assessing some of my analytical work, or simply providing an ear to absorb my various moans and complaints about the game, Jon's influence on both this book, and myself, cannot be underestimated.

A huge thanks can also go to the team at The Coaches' Voice, who have given me many wonderful years of analysing the game, and creating various football content. Tony Hodson and the team trusted me to come on board just after launch back in 2018, and it's been a pleasure to be associated with such quality content. I have certainly taken many skills and attributes from them all, which no doubt makes this book much stronger as a result.

Similar can then be said of all the individual coaches I have been paired with over the years. I have take so much from my time working with an outstanding range of talented staff and players at various clubs, pushing me to improve every single day.

Pitch Publishing has also been fantastic in helping me get this project over the line, in my first – and likely last – solo adventure. I thank them immensely for both the opportunity, and trust shown in my ideas.

Final thanks go to my closest family and friends who have always supported my professional goals and aims, and it never goes unnoticed who is consistently there for you when you do need them. This book is therefore dedicated to Mum, Shaun and Charlie, Dad, Charlene, and Olivia. The best coaching team anyone could ask for.

Introduction

IT HAS long been said within the coaching world that the best coaches are the best thieves. This book supports that notion entirely, taking a multitude of ideas, structures, principles, and tactics across the 2020/2021 Premier League season and hopefully providing an insight into the huge amount of detail and flexibility involved, and the level of utter genius at which the most elite head coaches frequently operate.

Unfortunately, not everything across the season can be covered, and not every team in the league will have a focused section, particularly from a season such as 2020/21 which will live long in the memory for reasons both on and off the field. However, the topic which almost all fans enjoy the most – scoring goals – will touch upon all 20 of the Premier League sides.

It's appreciated that not everyone reading this will be a coach, or an analyst of some sort. It can also be guaranteed that the terminology used will not be universal, even within the footballing world. Therefore, for clarity of understanding, certain phrases and ideas will be highlighted here prior to progressing on to the tactics and strategies themselves.

Most people are familiar with a football pitch's layout and shape. But for added detail and rationale, each diagram will be split into five vertical lanes. In some cases these are ordered numerically as one to five, but moving forward these vertical lanes will be described using specific terminology. The two outer lanes are classed as the 'Wide Areas', while the middle space running vertically from top to bottom is the 'Central Lane'. The two remaining areas are defined as 'Inside Channels'. Sometimes they are referred to

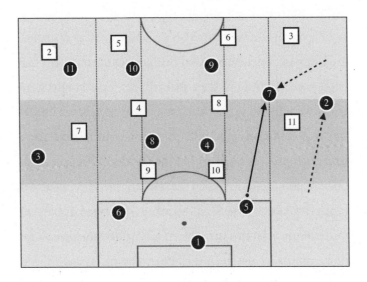

as the 'Half-Spaces', but that phrase has never really appealed to me.

With further regard to the diagrams themselves, the main team of focus will always appear from the bottom facing up. This is a relatively simple yet effective trick I learned as a coach. From the players' perspective, and now you, the reader, this is to prevent further confusion, keeping the left-back, for example, on the left-hand side of the board, and now diagram. For additional clarity, the specific team of focus will also appear as black circles, with the more generic opposition as white squares. Dashed arrows simulate player movements or dribbles if in possession of the ball, with solid arrows simulating a pass. On some diagrams players will be faded, indicating their starting position before performing a specific movement.

Players' numbers can also be a source of contention and debate within football. Here, they may appear different to what is seen elsewhere. Goalkeepers, as is universally accepted, are classed as 1, with the full-backs or wing-backs as 2 and 3. Central defenders will primarily appear as 5 and 6, with the defensive midfielder, also referred to as the single pivot on occasion, prioritised as number 4. Two defensive midfielders may also be referred to as a double pivot. The more offensive central midfielders are often assigned 8 and 10, with the right-winger at 7, left-winger at 11, and central forward at 9.

However, due to different base structures to begin with – such as two central forwards, back threes, midfield diamonds – the numbers may move around slightly. But the main aim is to again provide consistency, and then an explanation of the why behind the strategy, or idea. Various individual players in the same position will also demonstrate differing roles, positions, and ideas throughout the book, yet the same number for that position will apply where possible.

Should a full-back (2, 3) move into a central midfield position, for example, they will still hold the same number. The numbers on the diagrams also won't correspond to the players' actual squad numbers from the 2020/21 season. João Cancelo of Manchester City, for example, will always be 2, and not 27, his official Premier League number for the 2020/21 season, no matter which part of the pitch he moves into.

All open-play moments have been covered across the book, beginning with the attacking phase. This is split into three further chapters of build-up play, creating the attack, and then a brief look at the goals themselves. The two moments of transition, where possession of the ball changes between the two teams, follows as section two, with counter-attacking play, and then the transition into defence being the main points of focus.

The third and final section focuses on the prolonged defensive strategies, starting with pressing high up the pitch, moving into mid-block defending, and then a final overlook of the low block, and deep defending strategies. Although the moment of focus will take up the majority of the content, it will hopefully connect into various other moments in the game and not be viewed totally in isolation, particularly as the Premier League can be, at times, very chaotic.

1

Season 2020/21

THE COVID-19 virus halted Premier League football in March 2020 after Arsenal head coach Mikel Arteta returned a positive test. Leicester City's 4-0 victory over Aston Villa in game 288 of the 2019/20 season became the last Premier League action for some time. Four days prior, the first COVID death had been registered in the UK.

One hundred days after the events at the King Power Stadium, match 289 ignited Project Restart with Premier League football resuming as Aston Villa were again involved, this time holding Sheffield United to a relatively drab 0-0 at Villa Park. The match was arguably most memorable for a rare error involving Hawk-Eye's goal-line technology system.

The remaining 91 matches were played across June and July 2020, with zero fans, temperature checks, weekly testing of players and staff, and simulated crowd noise soon becoming the norm. Liverpool were crowned champions; Norwich City, Watford, and Bournemouth were relegated to the Championship and 2019/2020 was finally concluded.

Scheduling

The off-season has long been an essential aspect of the football calendar. Predominantly designed to provide enough rest for both staff and players, this period proves especially important for those involved in summer international tournaments. Between 2015 and 2019, the gap between Premier League campaigns averaged 88 days, providing ample physical and mental recuperation time before squads focused on a carefully planned fitness regime to best prepare for the season ahead.

Yet 2019/20 overran by 71 days – almost an entire off-season in itself – with the summer's European Championships also being postponed by a year. This left a break of just 49 days for both players and staff to recover from the disrupted yet still demanding campaign before then implementing a drastically shortened pre-season schedule prior to 2020/2021. Chelsea, Manchester City, Manchester United, and Wolverhampton Wanderers also had further European fixtures to complete after their domestic campaign had ended, giving them a further delay to their 2020/21 schedule.

Where possible, leagues will look to begin and finish seasons slightly earlier, allowing for an easier transition into summer tournaments. The three Premier League seasons prior to the COVID-19 disruptions lasted on average for 278 days each. But as the Premier League was forced into an extremely tight window to complete 2020/21, play was concluded within 254 days. Excluding the prolonged season of 2019/20, 2020/21 had the Premier League's latest finish since 2015, ending on 23 May 2021.

Despite the need for an early finish before any adaptation to the summer's rearranged European Championships, 2020/21 was played in an extremely condensed timeframe.

Players and staff were expected to deliver the highest standards of performance across a 380-game season – plus extra cup competitions thrown in – in this much shortened schedule, while coming off the back of a severely shortened rest period. With the 2022 World Cup in Qatar to be played in a reduced timeframe of 28 days towards the end of the year – the first World Cup to be completed outside of May, June, or July – coupled with the proposed expansion of events such as the UEFA Champions League, and the attempted

European Super League, COVID-19 further aggravated already tense scheduling issues.

The traditional football calendar over the festive period has long set English football apart from many other European leagues. However, the Premier League introduced a mid-season break in February 2019, allowing players and staff to recover after so many games in such a condensed timeframe, while still maintaining the traditional and often exciting festive period of matches. This break was scrapped for 2020/21.

With 2020/21 unable to offer a even a brief pause in fixtures, additional midweek matches were then crammed into an already shortened season. In the three seasons prior to COVID-19, the Premier League averaged 48 fixtures on a Tuesday, Wednesday, or Thursday, excluding Boxing Day, and New Year's Day matches. Through 2019/20 this increased to 64, albeit with the majority of these after Project Restart. The condensed 2020/21 then had 77 as teams frequently played three matches in seven days. In Manchester United's case, they were forced to play three Premier League games in just five days with only one rest day in between each one.

Injuries

Due to the tempo and speed of play at the highest level of professional football, a single match leads to acute fatigue, requiring several days to fully recover. Matches within a few days of one another, however, repeated over numerous weeks and months, quickly leads to chronic fatigue [1]. With the Premier League one of the most intense and fast-paced competitions around, the resting period is arguably just as important as the players' actual performances.

A study [2] found that 60 per cent of players who underperformed at the 2002 FIFA World Cup had played a mean of 12.5 matches in the ten weeks prior to the tournament, whereas players deemed to perform better than anticipated had played just nine times in the same period.

In 2010 it was found [1] that competing in the UEFA Champions League, and thus increasing the matches per week from one to two, increased the injury rate of players by more than six times. This was later confirmed [3] in a study focusing on 27 different teams, competing over 11 seasons. Total injury rates and muscle injury rates both increased in league matches with less than, or equal to, four days of recovery time, compared to at least six days of recovery.

According to premierinjuries.com, compared to the disrupted 2019/20 Premier League season there was a 23 per cent rise in muscular injuries over the first nine game weeks of 2020/21. Up to and including game week 21 through 2019/20, there were 356 injuries where players had to miss at least one league game. This number rose to 374 at the same point through 2020/21, and increased significantly to 435 when COVID-19-related absences were factored in.

Liverpool were particularly affected by injuries as by game week 26 players had been sidelined for a total of 1,032 days, with Crystal Palace the second worst off at that point in the campaign, with 864 days missed. As well as the lengthy onfield injuries best highlighted by the absentees within their central defence, several Liverpool players also tested positive for COVID-19 and were forced to isolate as a result. Despite having to close their training ground due to a COVID-19 outbreak in January 2021, Aston Villa had only missed 428 days though injury, the fourth lowest after the first 25 game weeks.

Substitutions

One new aspect of Project Restart saw the Premier League increase the amount of substitutions to five per match, with the bench also increasing to nine instead of the usual seven. However, this wasn't continued into 2020/21, and votes on three separate occasions from all 20 clubs failed to reach the 14 required for a change of law. The Premier League then became the only major league in Europe to return to three substitutions for the

2020/21 campaign, with five substitutes still in place for both the Champions League and Europa League. In England itself, the Premier League also stood alone as both the FA Cup and EFL Cup allowed five substitutions per game.

Although the bench increased back to nine after game week 14, and 'Additional Permanent Concussion Substitutions' were also introduced midway through the season, many head coaches were still frustrated at their inability to rotate multiple players mid-game.

When five subs were available after Project Restart, many teams often elected to use the new maximum on offer, with 80 per cent of teams using all five at least once. From the 92 matches in total, five subs were utilised at 32.1 per cent, and proved the most frequent selection. Four subs closely followed at 29.9 per cent, with fewer than three subs only used at 17.9 per cent across the remainder of the season.

Champions Liverpool utilised five subs more than any other option during their post-break matches, as did Bournemouth, Brighton & Hove Albion, Everton, Newcastle United, and Norwich City. These latter five clubs all finished in 12th place or below, and Burnley were the only side in the entire league to average fewer subs per match during Project Restart compared to the games prior.

Moving into the 2020/21 season, only two of the sides who finished in the top four were among the highest 11 for most substitutions made across the season – Liverpool and Chelsea. And from those same 11, six of these sides finished tenth or lower in the final table, with champions Manchester City using the lowest amount of substitutions across the season. The notion, then, that the extra substitutions rule only benefits the clubs towards the top of the table can certainly be challenged.

Home vs. Away

The theory of home advantage has long been known throughout professional football, with 'tough' away fixtures often predicted across the season. The impact of the home support has been proven to play a part in this as additional confidence and positivity within players' performances have been identified as key variables, obtained via that perceived advantage [4].

Looking at the three Premier League seasons prior to 2019/20, home victories accounted for 47.4 per cent of all results, with away wins averaging at 30.3 per cent. Stretching across the ten years prior, away wins averaged at just 28.7 per cent of matches.

Project Restart not only saw matches played behind closed doors, but also at an unprecedented schedule.

Games devoid of fans have often been associated with punishments, with crowds having been banned from attending due to clubs' wrongdoing. However, the COVID-19 pandemic stopped crowds gathering for all Premier League football, and they only returned momentarily during 2020/21.

A study [5] assessed whether the lack of social pressure from spectators affected behaviour and outcomes. It assessed 160 matches behind closed doors since the beginning of the 2002/03 European season prior to April 2020. A comparison with over 33,000 other matches showed that, on average, the home team won on 36 per cent of occasions without crowds, and 46 per cent with an audience. This was accompanied by a significant increase in away victories during behind-closed-doors matches, also accounting for fewer goals scored by the home sides. However, this study only focused on games in Italy and France due to the lack of such fixtures between 2002 and 2020 in the other top European leagues.

Prior to the COVID-enforced Premier League break, home win percentage averaged at 44.3 per cent. Post-break, this actually improved marginally to 48.7 per cent. However, similar results also appeared regarding away victories; before the pause in the schedule away wins stood at 30.2 per cent, whereas after it they only marginally improved to 32.2 per cent.

A cluster of games during December 2020 saw a maximum of 4,000 spectators attending a Premier League match, hosted by a club within the UK Government's Tier 1 region. Tier 2 then capped any attendance to a maximum of 2,000 fans, while Tier 3 and Tier 4 blocked all attendance completely. Crucially, in any region, away travel and support was still strictly prohibited.

Chelsea were the first club to welcome fans back to a Premier League match, beating Leeds 3-1 in front of 2,000 fans, with a handful of games then following over the coming weeks. However, after multiple reviews updating the tier locations, Liverpool and Everton became the final two clubs allowed to admit a select few before they too were forced to perform back in front of four empty stands. Premier League clubs were then allowed to welcome up to 10,000 home fans, or 25 per cent of a stadium's total capacity – whichever figure was lower – for the final two rounds of fixtures in 2020/21. Away support was once again prohibited.

Looking across the entire season, there were more away points won than home points for the first time in Premier League history, with 153 victories secured on the road. Compared to the 144 home victories, this proved a significant change as the highest number of away wins since 2010 in the Premier League had stood at 128 in 2018/19. Manchester United remained undefeated across all 19 away matches, while eight of the top ten won more points away from home than they did in their own stadiums. However, from the bottom half of the table, only four sides secured more away wins than at home. Although fans don't account for the entirety of the final result, the 2020/21 season has proved they certainly can contribute towards it.

The Referee

The absence of a crowd has also been shown to impact refereeing performances. A report [6] summarised that a home crowd can influence the decision-making of an official, specifically within a professional sporting context. It was also shown [7] that football fans themselves believe they do affect the outcome of matches, especially in favour of their own side, through the influencing of refereeing decisions.

Another report [5] found that behind-closed-doors matches provided significant differences in how the referees disciplined the away side. On average, visiting teams were awarded a third of a yellow card more per match when facing the presence of home support. However, this difference generally disappeared behind closed doors, suggesting that the referee can be affected by the social pressures provided by the dominance of home team support, and thus punishes the away side more severely.

A study [8] of 841 matches behind closed doors across the 2019/20 season, in the first and second divisions in England, France, Germany, and Spain, focused on the impact of crowd noise on both the home advantage, and any unconscious referee bias. The results suggested that home advantage was reduced compared to the average across the previous three seasons within the same competitions, but still existed. The referees did not reveal any bias favouring the home sides during these matches regarding fouls, bookings, penalties, or extra time awarded, indicating that this factor may be affected by the presence of the social pressures provided by home spectators.

Across the 2018/19 Premier League season there were 64 more yellow cards awarded to the away sides, with 62 during the disrupted 2019/20 season. However, that gap dropped significantly during 2020/21, with a difference of just 12. This drop was not repeated regarding red cards though, with the number awarded to away sides increasing very slightly through 2020/21.

VAR

The Video Assistant Referee (VAR) was introduced to Premier League football in 2019/20 to help minimise officiating errors through the use of supportive technology. Clubs unanimously approved the use of VAR into a second season, in line with the full FIFA VAR protocol. During its Premier League debut in 2019/20, VAR directly affected 109 goals or incidents across the 380 matches.

From these 109 overturned decisions, Newcastle United were the only side not to face a decision changed against their favour. Twenty-seven overturns led to goals, with 56 goals chalked off. Twenty-two penalties were awarded – nine of which were missed anyway – with seven penalties taken away after initially being awarded by the onfield officials. Thirty-four goals were ruled out for offside, with eight awarded after an incorrect offside decision prior. Fourteen goals were disallowed for handball and just two were allowed after a wrong handball decision. And finally, nine red cards were awarded through VAR, with three overturned after a second look.

VAR changed slightly for the 2020/21 season, with the referee making more use of the pitchside TV than before. Assistant referees also kept their offside flags down until the end of the attacking phase, whether that came from a goal, or as the ball went out of play for the attacking side. In the previous season, if a flag was raised it was up to the referee to stop the game. The

Premier League initially elected not to enforce VAR to check whether a goalkeeper had moved off his line during penalty kicks. However, through 2020/21 this was changed as goalkeepers were ruthlessly checked, and then booked on each offence after their first warning.

Moving into 2020/21, VAR directly affected 128 goals or incidents across the season, an increase of 19 from the year prior. Seven more goals were awarded, totalling at 34, with 42 then disallowed, a decrease of 14. Thirty-two of those ruled out were for an offside call, as seven were then awarded after an initial incorrect call regarding offside. A further six were ruled out for handball.

Seventeen red cards were awarded via VAR, with just two then overturned after an initial onfield dismissal. Three penalties were ordered to be retaken after a goalkeeper had encroached off his line. Wilfried Zaha, Mateusz Klich and Bruno Fernandes all then scored their subsequent second efforts.

In total, Burnley and Everton had the best net score regarding VAR overturns in their favour of +4 across 2020/21, with Arsenal, Liverpool, and West Bromwich Albion all suffering the most with a joint worst net total of -6 overturns against. Liverpool actually had 13 decisions overturned against them across the season, with a total of seven goals disallowed.

2

Building

ALL HEAD coaches want to control as many aspects of the game as possible. The word management itself stems from the Italian verb 'maneggiare', descended from the Latin 'Manus', meaning 'the hand'. This was often associated with control, and the ability to handle, but not in the handling the ball sense.

Playing out from the back, and building via multiple short passes deep inside the defensive third, has become a core strategy for many Premier League sides in recent seasons. Compared to the alternate method of playing more direct passes forward, where the odds of success are often 50/50, shorter build-up work can provide that craved control over specific passages of play and the moments that immediately follow.

Shorter build-up play is predominantly used to improve the quality of end product at the opposite end of the pitch. By luring the opposition forward through repeated shorter passing, spaces in behind the opponent's back line frequently increase. And depending on how organised the opposing units are in supporting one another, larger gaps can also develop.

But no tactic or strategy is flawless. The aftermath of losing possession within the defensive third, compared to after a long pass deep into the opponent's half, can be much more damaging. This, and the perception that both goalkeepers and defenders should prioritise their duties when out of possession – even at the expense of their attributes with the ball – will remain the strategy's biggest criticisms.

Yet from August 2017 to March 2020, goalkeeper kicks – open play, set pieces, and goal kicks – accounted for 79.1 per cent of all actions, with hand actions – throws, catches, punches, and saves – recorded at just 20.9 per cent within the Premier League. There can be no doubt that modern goalkeepers use their feet much more than their hands.

From goal kicks especially, playing out from the back has been made slightly easier for the side in possession. A rule change introduced to the Premier League during the 2019/20 season allowed team-mates to stand, and take possession, inside the penalty area directly from a goal kick. And with the offside law still temporarily suspended during this goal-kick pass, teams could better set up for a shorter first pass, *and* a direct ball in behind simultaneously, with opponents initially locked outside of the area.

Through 2019/20, most teams took advantage of this with 708 (25.1 per cent) of all 2,821 goal kicks being received inside the penalty area. Both Manchester clubs were the only sides who received more inside the area than outside, with Sheffield United the only club to not receive any inside the box. In 2020/21, the average length of goal kicks for the entire league shortened by five yards.

Leeds United secured promotion back to the Premier League in 2020, predominantly through Marcelo Bielsa's expansive playing style. A core aspect of his Leeds side that secured the Championship title – after losing out the season prior to Derby County in the play-offs – was persistent shorter build-up play. Predominantly using two main structures, 4-3-3 and the 3-3-1-3, Leeds' play out from the back under Bielsa has, for the most part, been clean, efficient, and, most importantly, heavily contributed to their eventual attacking play. Across Bielsa's first two seasons in England, his side secured the most penetrations into the opponent's half, the final third, and the opposing penalty area, and offered similarly impressive figures through 2020/21.

Many promoted teams naturally establish a defence-first mentality in their return – or debut – season in the top flight. Sheffield United in 2019/20 and Wolverhampton Wanderers in 2018/19 had two particularly impressive returning seasons, both finishing comfortably in the top half. However, they did so through organised and prolonged defending, with respective back-five structures and rarely playing out from the back, especially against other top-half opponents.

Leeds, on the other hand, not only managed a top-half finish in their return season but did so with an extremely positive and proactive playing style. None of the self-appointed 'Big Six' – who attempted to break away and form the European Super League – managed to win at Elland Road in 2020/21, and with the exception of Manchester City and Liverpool, no side penetrated into the opponent's half more than Bielsa's, stemming from their calm and controlled build-up.

Back-line Combinations

A common approach when playing out from defence is both centre-backs taking up very wide, and sometimes deep, starting positions. The full-backs then move forward into the next line as the big gap now created between the central defenders can be filled by a dropping midfielder, temporarily creating a back three. These wide centre-backs increase the pressing distance for the opposing centre-forwards while creating new spaces for team-mates in the second line to move, rotate, and receive in. Making the pitch big, then, is a common first objective when playing out from the back.

With depth secured by the centre-backs and goalkeeper, teams then expand the pitch through height and width. Height is usually dictated by the opposition, however, as the positioning of their back line, coupled with the offside law, restricts how high a front line can operate, except on the first pass from goal kicks. Width is therefore the most manageable aspect of the trio, and Leeds elected to create this primarily through their deep full-backs.

Whenever Leeds lost possession during build-up, the central defenders were better placed to protect the central spaces, instead leaving a weakened presence in the centre via a dropping midfielder. On the rare occasions when they converted mid-game from a back four into a trio, defensive midfielder Kalvin Phillips predominantly dropped around the outside of Leeds' two centre-backs. When possession was lost here, Leeds then had at least one central defender positioned in front of their goal instead of a dropping midfielder. Bielsa would primarily use the 4-3-3 structure across the 2020/21 season, with the occasional use of the 3-3-1-3. Only in the most extreme of cases did he switch between the two mid-game.

The use of one defensive midfielder was paramount in both structures, with a huge physical demand placed on this particular role. As the play moved across the back line, this single pivot performed frequent lengthy movements across the pitch. Constantly repositioning, this maintained a central passing lane straight through the opposing first line of pressure. When up against one central forward, Leeds' centre-backs frequently paused on the ball, luring them to one side before passing back across towards their central defensive partner. With the ball moving faster than any player can run, the central passing lane was then easy to access as long as Leeds' pivot had repositioned by moving across the pitch, in the same direction as the ball.

Two opposing central forwards naturally posed a bigger issue for Leeds' defensive midfielder, as the pair comfortably blocked forward passes from the centre-backs. Bielsa's 3-3-1-3 system was then preferred as the single pivot still now supported a back-line trio, with versatile wing-backs starting higher than the full-backs seen in the 4-3-3. The defensive midfielder then ceased their lengthy sideways movements, holding a more permanent position within the central lane instead.

Whenever the opposing forwards covered central passes, Leeds' wider centre-backs (4 and 6) broke the first line via a dribble forward. These aggressive drives through the inside channels or wide areas were supported by the wing-backs (2 and 3) outside of the ball, ready for close combinations. Stepping past the first line also opened access back across toward the defensive midfielder (8), once the ball was ahead of both opposing centre-forwards.

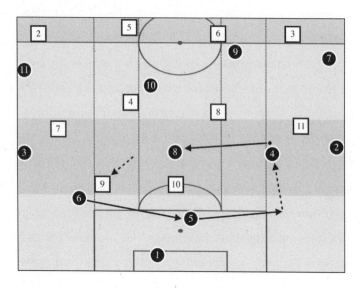

As the opposing first line would then widen to stop these dribbles, a central passing lane re-emerged to find the defensive midfielder (8) with passes penetrating between the first line. Pausing on the ball again helped to lure both centre-forwards across, especially from

Leeds' widest centre-backs. But it was crucial the back trio was staggered slightly, with the middle centre-back (5) positioned underneath the ball and not blocking a potential pass directly between the two wide centre-backs. The goalkeeper could also help to switch play between those two if needed.

Leeds' 4-3-3 was occasionally used when facing two central forwards. But when narrow wingers in the opponent's second line covered the inside channels, this stopped Leeds finding their central midfield overload and their centre-backs from stepping in. Forward progress then came via quick passing across the back line, and an especially powerful pass into the wide full-backs. If the initial pass was played with enough speed and accuracy, the full-backs could also drive past the opposing second line, now able to connect directly with the higher attackers. Bielsa spends a considerable amount of training time repeating specific patterns and movements. This meticulous work focuses on both tempo and timing, allowing strategies such as these to occur against a variety of opposition.

Against a front-line trio – the most common first line Bielsa faced through 2020/21 – Leeds utilised their 4-3-3 structure. From here, the depth and width provided by their full-backs (2 and 3) opened a first-time pass back inside, especially when opposing wingers pressed along the touchline, stopping the wide dribble forward via the full-backs. This first-time 'bounce' pass is used throughout Bielsa's methodology, and all over the pitch.

But specifically when breaking the first line, the bounce pass allowed the defensive midfielder (4) to receive from the closest side instead of constantly repositioning and moving across the pitch in what is already an extremely physically demanding role within Bielsa's playing style. As in these moments the opposing winger was close by, the pass across from the centre-back (5) was usually played into the safe side of the full-back (2), now bouncing the ball into the defensive midfielder (4) via their inside foot. The speed of this particular pass across was also slower than many of the

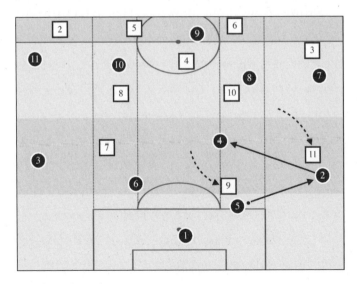

passes across the back line, better enabling a first-time pass from the full-back, while up against close pressure.

If the opposing winger pressed inwards, now working between Leeds' centre-back (5) and full-back (2), and the centre-forward still blocked the single pivot (4), a blindside run inside from the full-back (2) helped to break the first line. Prior to this run, the centre-back (5) took slightly wider touches, dragging the opposing winger further towards the wide area. This created a bigger gap to pass through, as the full-back (2) then drifted inside, receiving a disguised pass behind their direct opponent. A reverse of this combination saw the centre-back perform a disguised touch back towards the centre, before passing in front of the winger's inwards press, where the full-back could hold their wide position.

Depth from the full-backs also stretched the opponent's higher defending, significantly increasing the distance of press. As this positioning also created bigger gaps between the lines for Leeds' defensive midfielder to operate in, opponents soon prioritised defending the central areas. From here, Leeds' build-up focused on wider sequences, with a huge variety of impressive movements, patterns, and penetrative combinations breaking through higher defending.

Under Bielsa, Leeds have incessantly used one-twos and third-man run combinations to escape pressure within their own half, as well as when creating deep inside the opponent's half. Their wide full-backs (2) frequently lured the opposing winger to press from in to out, before then combining with a winger (7) dropping along the touchline. Although the one-two combination isn't particularly groundbreaking, the depth from the full-back's (2) starting position made the press longer for the opposing winger. This not only increased the space to receive a return pass – making it significantly easier to secure – but meant the opposing winger was lured to overcommit with a more aggressive press than necessary.

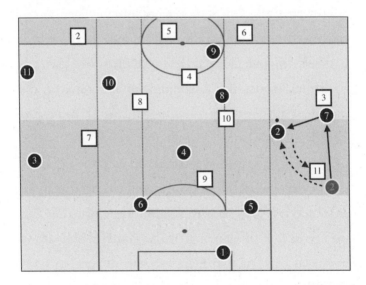

The full-back (2) superbly showcased their timing and connections here, holding the ball long enough to lure the opponent close before releasing into their dropping winger (7) and running inside in one fluid motion. Releasing the ball just before the opposing winger began to slow down also gave the full-backs a biomechanic advantage. By passing the ball in a similar direction as the eventual run, the full-backs could efficiently move forwards. Because the opposing winger had to stop, turn, and accelerate back in the opposite direction to their press, it was unlikely they'd reach the return pass back in time. With the Premier League played at such a high speed, the pressing wingers had little chance of stopping this combination.

Alternatively, whenever the opposing winger started much wider, cutting off the pass around, Leeds' winger (7) then dropped towards the inside channel. The full-back then made an overlapping run to receive on the outside, creating the same one-two combination, just slightly adapted.

But when the full-back combined with the defensive midfielder instead, their closest winger stayed away so as to not block the return pass into the full-back. The variety of just this one particular combination shows how well constructed Bielsa's session design has been across his tenure, as many of Leeds' players – especially those in the back line – aren't quicker than most opposing wingers they face. But due to their excellent timing, they persistently combined their way through or around opposing pressure, and quickly adapted to any changes in opposing pressure.

Third-man combinations offer an extra layer to the one-two sequence, with Leeds still focusing on returning the ball back to the player who began the move, ideally now positioned beyond the next opposing line. But Bielsa's side would also use third-man combinations to find specific players in key spaces, most notably their single pivot (4).

To prohibit the wider one-two combinations, the opposition's central midfield blocked the inside channel as the wingers also covered access back inside where possible. Leeds' wide full-back (2) then lacked the space to receive a return pass after making their

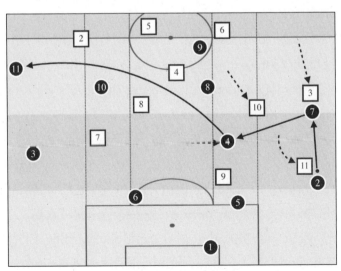

run forward. But as the opposition prioritised this first pass they struggled to cover the single pivot (4), especially as they moved towards the ball at the last minute.

Leeds' build-up then continued along the touchline and into the dropping winger (7). But instead of the full-back (2) moving forward to receive, the winger bounced the ball first-time into the defensive midfielder (4), who could either continue a combination on the same side or switch the play, where the other wide full-back (3) and winger (11) pairing was ready to attack. Whenever the opposition's central forward deepened to cover in front of the defensive midfielder (4), Leeds simply switched across their back line via the central defence, before attempting to combine in the other wide area.

Leeds also adopted more assertive third-man combinations without the need to switch the play. But with the opposition still covering the spaces close to the ball, the wider defenders now made longer runs forward as Bielsa's side penetrated with more direct forward passing.

Instead of holding their position after releasing the ball against an outward press, the full-backs (2) followed their line pass into the dropping winger (7). Whenever the opposing full-back tightly followed to stop the winger (7) from turning, space opened up for the full-back (2) to receive in behind. If they didn't perform this press, then the winger (7) could turn freely, and attack.

If the full-back (2) started much deeper, and thus had a longer run to move in behind, the receiving winger (7) was forced to hold possession for longer, increasing the emphasis on hiding and shielding the ball, often using one foot on it and the opposite arm to hold off the opponent. The release of pass was then delayed, usually until the full-back (2) had at least moved in line with the ball.

To stop the final pass in behind from being intercepted, it was essential it was delivered first-time, whether via the single pivot (4) or attacking midfielder (8). But should the full-back (2) start much closer to their winger partner (7), then this combination was often performed with multiple first-time passes with all players involved as the full-back could move in behind to receive much quicker.

Whenever opposing wingers pressed inwards from a wider starting position, they blocked this first pass along the touchline. Leeds' full-back then passed inside into the defensive midfielder, with the winger now the secondary link. If the winger was already positioned inside then their full-back partner continued to overlap

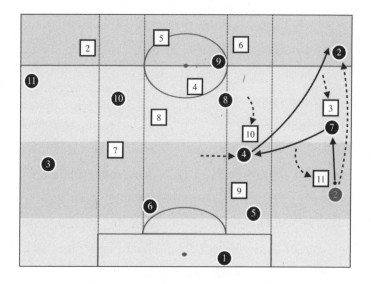

on the outside. But if the winger held the width then space was only available for the full-backs to underlap through the inside channel, following their pass into the single pivot, who was now positioned marginally further away from the ball, better encouraging the full-back to underlap.

In these moments, the defensive midfielder again delayed their release of pass until the full-back had moved into position. During this particular combination, the receiving full-back would often have to break through the opposing block via their first touch instead of running on to a lengthy through ball. This was because the direction of the third and final pass now released by the winger no longer matched the direction of the full-back's run, unlike when the single pivot made a forward pass in behind, mirroring the direction of the run provided by the full-back.

Fluid Second Line

Within Leeds' second line, the fluidity, height, and supporting movements provided by the two attacking midfielders gave further assistance to their build-up play. Because the single pivot was positioned deep towards the back line, and the attacking midfielders close to the front trio, Leeds often built with an outfield 5-5 strategy. When Bielsa utilised the 3-3-1-3 structure, however, this provided a more aggressive 4-6 format with the back three and single pivot deep, and the remaining players positioned high, providing multiple forward runs off the ball.

When facing a mid-block defensive strategy, Leeds' first line naturally built under less initial pressure, with the movements ahead of the ball growing in importance. Traditionally within a 4-3-3 structure, the two attacking midfielders position themselves through the inside channels with one on each side of the pitch. Yet Leeds demonstrated a much more fluid central unit through 2020/21, regularly changing their positioning ahead of the more fixed single pivot.

These movements created additional central passing lanes for the back line and defensive midfielder to break through the congested block. Swapping sides helped Leeds' attacking midfielders lose their individual marker, simply moving from one inside channel to the other, before receiving. Movements from high to low (10) provided bounce passes across the pitch, often into team-mates who were initially blocked off. Meanwhile, runs from low to high (8) focused on a more penetrative receiving style, with the central midfielders now facing forwards and able to drive straight at the opposing back line as the ball was received across the body, offering better protection from pressure from their individual marker. When changing both sides and heights with one movement, Leeds' attacking midfielders were especially hard to track.

These movements from the attacking midfielders also provided an important antidote for when the

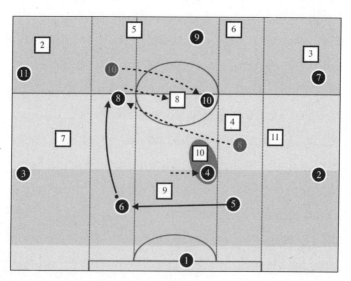

opposition placed a permanent marker on to the defensive midfielder (4). In these moments, the pivot (4) stopped offering wide for a pass from the centre-back (5), keeping the inside channel free. On occasions they would even move in the opposite direction to the pass across the back line, allowing the centre-back (6) further space for a vertical pass into the rotating attacking midfielder (8), or to dribble forwards if needed. As the defensive midfielder dragged their opponent away from the traditional pivot space, one of the attacking midfielders could drop even deeper than before and receive from the back line. If this longer run was aggressively tracked then it opened higher spaces for a team-mate to receive further forward, with a run from low to high. But when the attacking midfielder dropped unattached, they could turn, and progress the play whichever way they saw fit.

Whenever Bielsa did utilise a 3-3-1-3, Leeds utilised the attacking midfielders in two distinct ways. The first method involved the single pivot (4) dropping into the back line, as both full-backs (2 and 3) then moved forward. The two attacking midfielders then split, with one becoming the base of the midfield (8) as the predominant single pivot, linking with the back three and goalkeeper. The other attacking midfielder (10) then took up a higher role, often working alongside the central forward (9) as Leeds occupied both opposing central defenders.

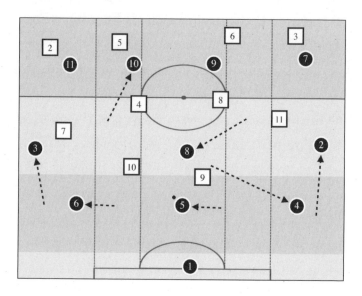

This rotation naturally had a huge effect on the positional requirements of the attacking midfielders. It no longer became about their rotations and fluid movements, but much more about their qualities on the ball in their new roles. The deepest of the two (8) was now more responsible for deeper build-up work, playing off limited touches, and constantly readjusting their positioning to support the back line behind the two central forwards, just as the single pivot in Bielsa's 4-3-3 showcased via sideways runs across the pitch. They also had to delay and cover any loss of possession, often acting as another central defender and particularly helping the now middle centre-back (5) in this regard.

Leeds' second rotation into 3-3-1-3 came as the original defensive midfielder (4) remained ahead of the back line, with just one full-back (3) now stepping into the next line. The attacking midfield pair once again split off into their new roles, with one moving forward (10) to support the central striker again. However, with the single pivot (4) still in place, Leeds then placed their second attacking midfielder in the wider areas (8), now as a connector to support the combinations between the reserved full-back (2) and winger (7).

The positional requirements once again changed for this specific role, with increased demands on one

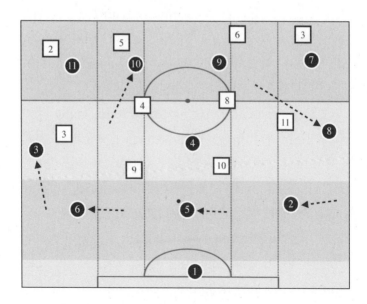

vs. one play in the wide areas as well as providing more vertical off-the-ball runs, assisting their two team-mates through the wide areas both during build-up, and after any losses of possession.

Not only did these fluid systems showcase Bielsa's variety of build-up methods, but also the versatility of the central midfield unit at his disposal. They were asked to perform a variety of roles across the season against the highest standard of opponent, while also covering an immense amount of ground in the process. Stuart Dallas was superb in this regard.

Leeds' attacking midfielders also contributed heavily to many of the wider rotations previously mentioned from the 4-3-3 structure. When the back line and defensive midfielder occasionally required an extra team-mate to combine with, the attacking midfielders often provided that additional support during both the one-twos and third-man combinations.

The most penetrative and direct run came after the winger's (7) dropping movement towards the ball had pulled the opposing full-back out of line. Space then emerged for the closest attacking midfielder (8) to run in behind. To nullify Leeds' wide full-backs, and their underlapping one-twos especially, many opposing wingers focused on shutting off the inside channel. This provided a small amount of extra time on the ball for the full-backs, especially as opposing wingers often had to reposition.

This enabled the winger (7) to drop further – now as a decoy movement rather than as a receiver – as the attacking midfielder (8) could begin their run beyond. A direct, bending pass over from the full-back (2) then found the closest attacking midfielder (8) moving into the opponent's half. If the opposing full-back then tracked this run, the winger (7) was free to receive, turn, and drive forward. Because of the extra time on the ball, the full-back (2) could better control their decision-making and change their release of pass at the last minute if needed.

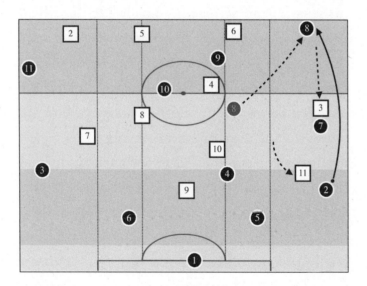

This forward run was also found via a first-time pass around the corner, usually from Leeds' defensive midfielder, should the opposing winger shut off the wide area and thus block any bending pass around. It was crucial that the pivot recognised that space in behind the opposing full-back was open, but the full-back couldn't access it themselves. So they then moved towards the ball, and as long as the pass back inside from the full-back was soft enough to encourage a first-time pass, but hard enough to still reach their team-mate, this pass around the corner could then find an identical forward run made by the closest attacking midfielder.

With the attacking midfielders both occupying the same side on occasions – usually after their fluid movements to receive – a second forward run supporting this bending pass around gave Bielsa's side another penetrative threat. This came in response to either the opposing defensive midfielder tracking the first run forward, or the central defence sweeping across to meet the runner's first touch. This second forward run from Leeds' farthest attacking midfielder helped to pin the central defender, and for the most part, stopped them from covering across. Should the opponent's defensive midfielder then fail to track the first run, the closest attacking midfielder received the pass unchallenged. This second run also allowed the receiving attacking midfielder to flick the ball on, should the pass from the full-back be played in the air and prove difficult to control while running forward at a high speed.

Along with running forward, the attacking midfielders also moved sideways to support wider combinations. When up against a flat midfield foursome, Leeds had a three vs. two central midfield overload, and they often took advantage of this as one of the attacking midfielders took up a very wide position, supporting between the full-back (2) and winger (7). This added an extra presence to both the one-twos and third-man combinations, while keeping their wingers high to attack the spaces in behind.

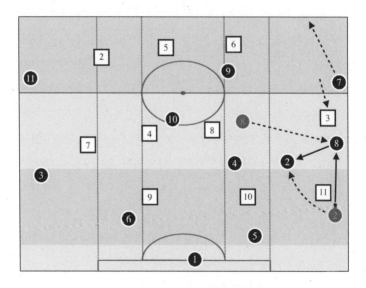

A particularly frequent combination saw Leeds' closest attacking midfielder (8) move wide and create the one-two combination with the underlapping full-back (2). Should the opposing full-back jump on to Leeds' attacking midfielder (8), then the combination often resulted in sliding the winger (7) in behind via the inside-running full-back (2). Whereas when they held their ground, the attacking midfielder (8) turned and drove forward themselves. As opponents soon followed this wide run, Leeds' other two central midfielders (4 and 10) found themselves free to receive and create central attacks, or switch the play.

The attacking midfielders also contributed to third-man patterns, albeit in a position not as wide as when assisting a one-two combination. Depending on how the opposing winger pressed, the full-backs either played line passes into a dropping winger to then bounce into the closest attacking midfielder, or inside passes against a wide opposing winger to find the attacking midfielder through the inside channel, to then bounce into their winger team-mate. This pattern was naturally much less penetrative compared to the play in behind, or over, but it still enabled Leeds to break the opponent's first line and then find a team-mate, often unattached, and receiving behind an opposing screener.

The final movements of support from the attacking midfielders came when dropping towards the ball, and thus coming short to receive. A third-man combination again proved useful when opposing wingers screened access between the centre-backs and full-backs, before pressing the ball. The defensive midfielder (4) once again stayed away from the ball, freeing the inside channel and allowing the attacking midfielder (8) to drop towards the centre-back (5). And as the ball was released, the full-back (2) began their forward run, ready to receive a bounce pass.

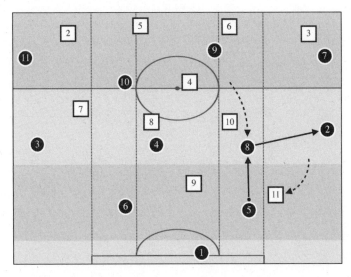

This dropping run often came from a high starting position, making it more difficult for the direct opponent to track and cover the movement. The pass from the centre-back (5) was often released before the receiving midfielder (8) was yet to fully drop. This ensured that when they did receive goalside of their opponent, the ball had only just arrived and could lure in the opponent, opening the space for the receiving full-back (2).

But when up against a high pressing strategy which involved the central forward screening Leeds' pivot, and the wingers pressed inside on to the centre-backs, this wider combination struggled. Although the attacking midfielders still dropped deep to bounce wide, the zonal defending from the opposing central midfield trio and intelligent covering from the outside shoulder prohibited Leeds' preferred combinations. To get through this press, Leeds converted from their 4-3-3 into their 3-3-1-3, flattening the opponent's first line and then better accessing their higher central players in the process.

The attacking midfielders would also drop short when the pivot had a permanent man-marker, as they moved away to vacate the central spaces in front of the back line. Although Leeds' defensive midfielder would then drag their opponent far away from the ball – usually high up the pitch – it was uncommon for the opposition to also man-mark their attacking midfielders, particularly the one who then dropped deep to receive.

With the central midfield unit so fluid and different across each match, it proved an almost impossible task to track and mark each and every one of Leeds' impressively coordinated movements as they would eventually find a way to progress the ball into the opponent's half.

High Front Line

For the most part, Bielsa's front trio was used to pin the opposing back line and provide the height element of the deeper build-up. The wingers would also provide extremely wide positions during build-up, even as the corresponding full-backs also began wide. In support of the wide combinations, Leeds' central forward would often move on to the closest centre-back, stopping them from stepping across as defensive cover while also creating diagonal passes back inside. The opposite winger would then narrow, occupying the space inside of the farthest opposing full-back.

Whenever Leeds' attacking midfielders were unable to provide the penetrative forward runs, the central forward (9) supported the more direct combinations through the wide areas. By offering beyond the dropping winger (7), the centre-forward became the primary receiver from their deeper full-back (2). But from their direction of run, it became difficult to progress the play as they approached the pass side on, instead of running from deep and thus directly following the trajectory forward, as the attacking midfielders could. Therefore,

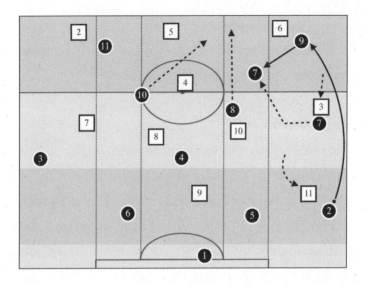

they needed an additional runner to create a bounce pass combination.

This latter support came either via the winger (7) inverting after their initial dropping movement, or from one of the attacking midfielders (8 and 10). The winger's movements were relatively straightforward because as soon as the pass cleared over their head, they spun inside of their opponent, ready to receive through the inside channel. Should the closest central defender cover across towards the central forward (9), then a larger gap emerged for the winger to receive, now as the third-man. From here they could drive with the ball, or attack by sliding the centre-forward in behind, merging the third man combination with a one-two movement. It was common across the 2020/21 season that Bielsa's side performed so many differing variants of combinations, some of them blended into one longer attacking move. But the timings and principles remained throughout.

Alternatively, one of the attacking midfielders (8, 10) would support the pass into the centre-forward. How the opposing defensive midfielder covered the central spaces then affected which one of the two midfielders made the run forward, with the detail of pass into the centre forward (9) heavily influenced as a result. If the centre-forward was under immense pressure, or the pass forward implied that it should be played first-time – a knock-down from a high aerial pass for example – then the closest attacking midfielder (8) made the central run of support. This was to ensure that the final pass now well within the opponent's defensive block was secured, with Leeds' farthest attacking midfielder (10) too far away to secure a first-time set.

But when the centre-forward (9) either received passes along the ground, or found themselves under less immediate pressure, they could now connect into the farthest attacking midfielder (10). Blindside runs around the opposing pivot, and then across the farthest centre-back, enabled the centre-forward to play either a ball in behind or a pass into feet, indicating a one-two combination back towards the centre-forward.

From Bielsa's 3-3-1-3 structure, the central forward was partnered by a high attacking midfielder. This meant permanently moving over to one side as opposed to supporting build-up play through both wide areas in the 4-3-3 structure. Round-the-corner passes from Leeds' expansive second line proved invaluable when connecting into the two highest central attackers (9 and 10). Passes from the widest defender were played dependent on the angle of pressure provided by the opposing winger, or closest central forward.

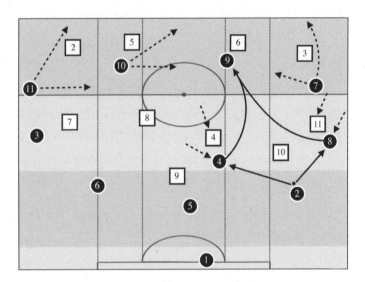

If access into the wide area was open then Leeds worked the ball around the opposing block, with the wide receiver playing a first-time pass across their body. As the receiving player in Leeds' second line initially dropped towards the ball, their direct marker often followed.

This helped to create more space between the lines for the eventual receiver. When an inward press was performed, forcing the wider centre-back inside, then the defensive midfielder (4) showed to receive between the opponent's first line. Their movement towards the ball also lured their direct opponent, again creating more space between the lines for Leeds' highest central attacker to receive and then combine with the multiple forward runs provided by the remainder of the front line.

If this round-the-corner pass lacked conviction, either through an initially inaccurate first pass from the wide centre-back (2), a poor connection from the second line (4), or a mistimed movement across from the high receiver (9), the fact that Leeds had two central threats high up the pitch meant they could still make something from it.

Once the play had bypassed the opponent's first two lines, it was then the job of the receiver (9) to secure the first contact, shielding and protecting what was often a bouncing ball. From here, forward runs beyond from both wingers (7 and 11) and the non-receiving high attacker (10) helped drag defenders away from the ball, isolating the closest opposing centre-back one vs. one. When the receiving attacker (9) escaped their opponent, multiple runs in behind from differing angles also proved a useful method of further progression via through passes.

But when penetration in behind wasn't available due to a narrow and compact back line blocking a potential through ball, inside movements from the two wingers (7 and 11) created bounce passing opportunities for Leeds' central threats (9 and 10). From here, the two highest attackers could both spin off together, with the wingers now in control of the move. Diagonal dribbles across the pitch from the winger (7 and 11) then created more penetrative moments for Leeds, with their most effective forward runners all ready to attack.

3

Creating

ONCE PLAY has progressed up the pitch, teams then look to create goalscoring chances, predominantly for the front line. Chances can come from direct forward play from back to front, or from patient build-ups, and much longer attacking sequences building through each third of the pitch. Chances can also stem from higher defending, and capitalising on opposition errors.

The main principles to create an attack involve movement, support, creating space, penetrating forward, and creativity. When in possession, teams can attack with play through an opposing block, around the outside, or directly over the defensive structure, depending on what strategy the opposition select.

During the 1998 World Cup and 2000 European Championships, France – who won both tournaments – made 81.3 per cent of their assists from Zone 14, the central area just outside of the penalty area. With the 4-4-2 formation being particularly common around that era, spaces beyond the opposing midfield unit were prime for receiving in and then feeding the front line from. Permanent defensive midfielders soon helped to cover access into this space, with the rise of the double pivot further blocking central access. Although many assists have continued to stem from Zone 14 (101), as the 2019/20 figures below show, play around the opposing defensive block has subsequently grown in importance.

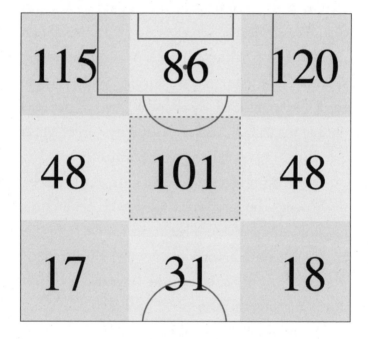

From here, the role of the goalscoring winger or wide forward has increased in importance within the

Premier League, often involving wrong-footed wingers, i.e. a left-footer attacking from the right and vice versa. Instead of driving around the outside, these players now prefer to cut inside and combine with central team-mates, or more often than not, shoot directly at goal. Twenty players scored more than ten Premier League goals in 2020/21, with 11 of these predominantly attacking as a wide forward and looking to cut inside.

Brighton & Hove Albion were promoted to the Premier League in 2017 and survived in their first two seasons under head coach Chris Hughton. Graham Potter then took over for 2019/20 after impressive spells with both Swansea City in the Championship, and Östersunds FK in the Swedish first tier. Potter led Brighton to 15th in his debut season in England's top flight, recording their best Premier League points tally yet.

For two consecutive seasons under Potter, Brighton have provided the biggest difference between the actual numbers of league goals scored and their expected goals return, indicating that they have created a significant amount of high-quality chances across both campaigns but have failed to convert them into goals scored. Brighton's final placing of 16th in 2020/21 came after 40 league goals across the season which could, and possibly should, have been closer to the 64 mark, making them the fourth highest in the league regarding expected goals for the season.

Creating Through

Brighton were predominantly set up in a back-three structure in 2020/21, paired with two defensive midfielders. Two wing-backs then provided the attacking width, supporting around an extremely flexible and fluid front line.

It was relatively rare that Brighton struggled to break the opposing first line. With the wing-backs around the outside, and the double pivot central, Potter's three centre-backs had multiple options to progress forward. But if the double pivot was blocked off then the back line increased the central spaces for the defensive midfielders to receive in, by circulating the ball across the pitch.

A backwards pass from wing-back to wide centre-back triggered the middle centre-back to drop off considerably, opening quicker access between the two widest centre-backs. A purposefully slower pass back from the wing-back often lured the opposing front line to press forward though, thus increasing the space their defensive midfielders could then receive in.

Depending on how the opposition set their midfield structure, where possible Brighton looked to match the number of gaps in the opposing second line with the same number of central passing options through. This provided Brighton's ball carrier with multiple forward passing options, allowing for more creativity, less predictable play, and frequent forward progression. An opposing midfield unit of four, for example, has three gaps. Brighton then utilised their front-line trio to offer through all of these three gaps at once, with the wing-backs as additional options around if needed.

When an opposing line or unit is flat, the gap between them and the next line is at its maximum, with one pass easily breaking an entire unit, whereas a slightly staggered defensive unit can reduce the spaces between the two lines. This also allows earlier pressure on to the receiving attacker, limiting their decision-making and future actions on the ball. Brighton's use of two defensive midfielders enabled them to quickly change the angle of pass into their front line, efficiently working the ball across the central areas before penetrating forward. This was often achieved before the opposing midfield could restructure, taking advantage of those times when an opponent individually pressed forward, but their closest team-mates then failed to narrow and cover behind this individual advance. No single pivot could recreate this changing of angle from Brighton's perspective as they regularly looked to deploy two players within their second line, even after various rotations.

These central gaps increased to four whenever the opposition deployed five players in their second line. Brighton then pushed one of their two defensive midfielders (8) beyond to accompany the front trio (9, 10, 11) between the lines, maintaining the many central passing options. This forward movement was often performed as the play moved through the opposite inside channel, allowing the farthest defensive midfielder (8) to move forward and reposition on the opponent's blind side. The corresponding wide centre-back (6) then moved forward slightly, temporarily pushing into Brighton's own second line, recreating the double pivot to help change the angle of pass through.

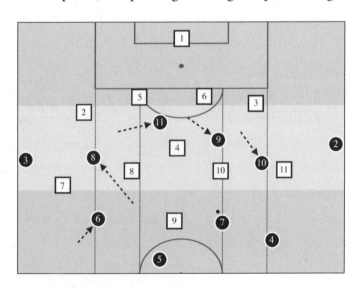

One of Brighton's double pivot would also drive forward with the ball, now breaking the opposing second line via a dribble instead of receiving a pass through. The ability to beat players one vs. one and break lines through dribbles is arguably the best tactic-breaker there is, often creating an instant overload while also taking opposing players out of the defensive equation. This is why players with a high dribble success rate are absolutely priceless, and can drastically alter the course of most matches.

This driving-through soon benefited Brighton's front line as an opposing defender was forced to engage with the dribbler, thus leaving an attacker unmarked, or at least under less pressure. Should the opposition stay with their original men, Brighton's ball carrier would continue the drive forward unchallenged. So although it proves more difficult to break the second line via a dribble, if successful, the rewards after penetration are often far greater.

To further assist breaking through centrally, one of Brighton's defensive midfielders would swap with one of the front line, maintaining the team's impressive presence behind the opposition's second line while also getting one of their more creative talents to initiate the central penetration. Potter's use of two attacking midfielders supporting a single central forward enhanced this particular rotation, giving Brighton two players who could alternatively and unpredictably drop deep, and break the lines via a penetrative dribble.

This dropping movement proved so effective as it displaced the opposing central midfielder, especially when the attacker dropped across the opponent's eye line. The initial defensive reaction was often to follow this first movement, temporarily creating a bigger gap to pass through, if Brighton could change the angle via their second line. Torn between following this run further and allowing the gap to increase further, or holding their ground but letting Brighton's dropping forward receive and turn freely, opposing midfielders battled this positional dilemma all season.

In order to penetrate through a particularly compact or a well-staggered second line, passes were hit firmer than usual, minimising the chance of interception. Although Premier League players – Brighton's included – are among the top of their profession, receiving a pass hit with such power over a relatively short distance can still prove challenging, particularly when also facing immediate pressure from both in front and behind – and possibly from the side – as opponents quickly condense against almost all attempted central play.

Therefore, in these moments a bounce pass helped Brighton's initial receiver (9) maintain possession after the line was broken. Releasing the ball first-time quickly worked the ball into a team-mate (10, 11) who faced forwards, while avoiding the first moments of defensive pressure. For the most part, Brighton's first receiver (9) bounced the ball using their closest foot, safely keeping it at the maximum distance from the defender approaching from behind, ensuring it frequently reached a team-mate (10, 11). But this did limit the receiver's ability to then spin off and receive in behind as a pass across the body via this front foot limited the hips from turning forward.

Although a bounce pass using the back foot encourages the defender to jump out and engage, it also allows the receiver to turn more after the release. Within this specific area of the pitch, further runs in behind could have been beneficial, especially if an opposing central defender had been lured out by via this back-foot technique.

An alternate bouncing method came when the central gaps were too narrow to play through, as Brighton worked the ball around the opposing second line and into their wing-backs (2, 3), before then bouncing the ball back inside. Although the receiving wing-back only had one realistic option to play into, as the closest attacker (10 or 11) blocked their team-mates, this still proved a useful strategy for Brighton to

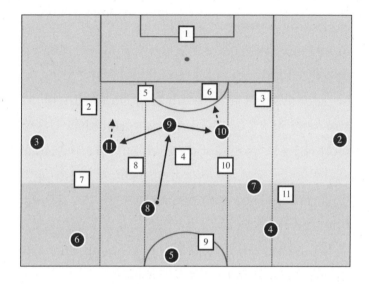

maintain their attacking territory and frequent access into the players placed between the lines.

Once the midfield line was broken, especially with a pass, well-coordinated movements furthered Brighton's ability to create chances on goal. Whether Potter selected two central forwards supported by a single attacking midfielder, or just one central forward flanked by two attacking midfielders, the entire front line performed runs both towards and away from the ball, acting as the first receiver or a secondary runner. And because of this fluidity and frequent interchange within Brighton's front line, it was rare that the same players made the same runs.

The two widest members of Brighton's trio at any given point (9, 11) often bent their runs in behind and around the outside of the opposing centre-backs, aiming to pull them away from their midfield line. This then increased the space in which the central member of the three attackers (10) could receive, also increasing the chance of a turn forward. These two bending runs beyond were also performed away from the central defender's eyeline, making it difficult to watch both the ball and track the movements simultaneously.

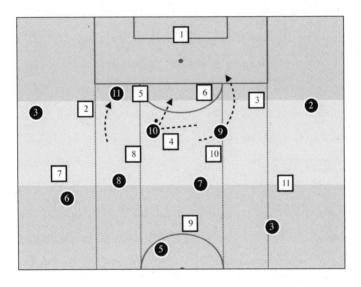

Brighton's central play was furthered as two of the trio (9, 10) also swapped roles and rotated prior to receiving the pass through. Double movements, most notably moving short before then spinning in behind the back line, also displaced opposing central defenders, the Seagulls then exploiting through that particular gap. The wing-backs were still on hand through the wider areas as secondary support when needed, even though the front trio naturally wanted to keep the ball central, especially once the opposing second line had been broken.

Another impressive aspect of Brighton's attacking play came through their decision-making and timing of release. Naturally, the objective for Brighton once breaking through the second line was to penetrate into the spaces in behind. Prior to this, however, the forwards often faced the most aggressive and compact defensive pressure.

But instead of staying on the ball for too long, eventual releases into the wider areas also proved effective to then combine, create, and deliver from the inside channels and wider areas. Brighton's front line was efficient at this 'hold and release' throughout the season, and struck the balance particularly well between luring defenders and then exploiting emerging spaces, without regular losses of possession.

In the moments where Brighton set their front line early, and the runner from deep moved ahead of the ball well before forward progress had been initiated, the opposition frequently narrowed their second line. Even if Brighton timed this rearrangement well, repeated central play also condensed the opposition's midfield line. Either way, the gaps to play through shortened considerably. Yet the opposition had to concede space somewhere. And with Brighton already locking the opponent into their half, and space in behind for play over relatively limited, the opposition's narrowing midfield unit relinquished space in the wider areas, with Brighton still able to create from here without having to adapt their style or structure.

Creating Around

Similar to when creating passing options through the central areas, Brighton ensured they had a presence within all the gaps of the opposing back line, ready to attack crossing deliveries, albeit now this presence focused on forward runs and finishing from balls across the penalty area, as opposed to the static receiving of forward passes.

When facing a back four, Brighton's narrow front trio provided runs through each of the three gaps within the opponent's back line, with the farthest wing-back supporting on the outside shoulder of the far opposing full-back, covering any overhit deliveries. One of Brighton's defensive midfielders would also provide cut-back support in front of the opposition's back line, keeping the more proficient front-line finishers attacking the spaces beyond as often as possible.

If one of the front line had been active during the early stages of the move forward, and was now unlikely to provide a central run in behind, they remained deep as the cut-back option. Brighton then provided an alternate runner from elsewhere, ensuring they still had at least three central runners as often as possible. For the most part it was the closest defensive midfielder (7) who replaced the dropping forward (10), primarily because this particular player had the shortest distance to reach Brighton's front line. This wasn't quite a fluid rotation between the two players though, instead performed through two more isolated movements.

When the forward (10) had dropped early, they often did so to combine with the wing-back (2) and instigate wider progress, or even deliver the cross themselves. The closest defensive midfielder (7) moved forward as the play was developing, often taking advantage of the dropping forward's (10) luring of the opposing central midfielder. This blindside run was timed to arrive within, and eventually through, the opposing back line as the ball was delivered back inside. This helped the runner remain onside, while maintaining their momentum ready for a leap against the centre-backs.

A slight delay to this particular run also allowed Brighton's remaining two forwards (9, 11) to reposition if needed, proving particularly useful for the central attacker (9), who could make runs across the first centre-back and attack lower crossing deliveries towards the front post.

Alternatively, the far wing-back (3) would move inwards, and attack within the opponent's back line instead, as opposed to covering from the opposite wide area. This occurred when the closest double pivot (7) was more active with the wider progression, providing further support to the dropping forward (10), and also delivering crosses when needed, but therefore unable to reach the front line via a run forward.

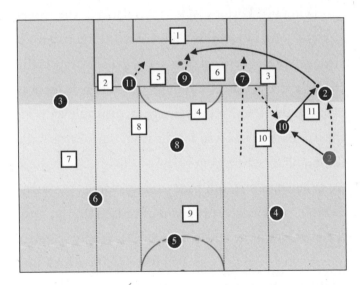

But the distance for the incoming wing-back (3) to move inside was fairly limited, realistically only able to attack between the far full-back and centre-back by the time the cross was released. Therefore, the duo remaining in Brighton's front line (9, 11) moved towards the ball and into a different gap.

If the opposing back line was well lined up then these runs were performed in front of their direct opponent, usually limiting the forwards to flicked finishes across their body. However, if the opposition's defence lacked organisation and one player played Brighton's front line onside, then blindside runs behind their marker could enable a much wider range of finishes, often meeting the ball much closer to goal.

Although Potter's side then lacked the cover beyond for any overhit deliveries, they did have a stronger presence to attack aerial crosses, especially those targeted towards the far post. Dan Burn was particularly effective in this regard, also able to work the ball back across goal for the front line to attack the second phase when appropriate.

When opposing full-backs tightly marked the wing-backs, or aggressively pressed outwards to stop an early cross, Brighton needed an extra runner beyond. Similar movements were also required when facing a back line of five, with the presence of the extra defender also limiting early crossing play.

Brighton's wider centre-backs then made underlapping runs forward to exploit this space beyond the opposing full-back, with the winger or forward opponent often unwilling to track this movement, especially as the defender frequently ended up crossing towards the byline. Brighton's closest forward (10) then moved on to the outside shoulder of the first centre-back, pinning them in place, with the central forward (9) dropping to perform a similar job on the opposing defensive midfielder. This helped limit any wider cover on to Brighton's receiving wide centre-back (4), meaning if an opponent still chose to cover the pass in behind they'd have to leave their original man free. Brighton's closest defensive midfielder (7) also provided similar pinning movements within the second line.

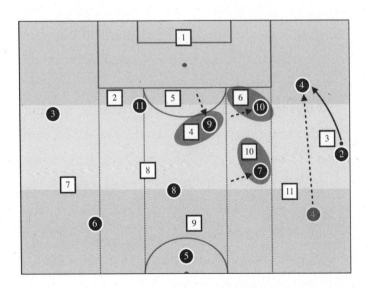

When direct access from the wing-back (2) into the underlapping wide centre-back (4) was blocked, the positioning of both Brighton's closest defensive midfielder (7) and forward (10) also created a third-man pass into the wide centre-back (4), using a front-foot pass to set the ball away from their opponent.

In place of the wide centre-back, the closest defensive midfielder (7) also made underlapping runs beyond. The wide centre-back (4) then narrowed, temporarily forming the double pivot in their place. Although this predominantly acted as transitional cover should the move break down, it also helped switch the play and change the angle of attack if wide progress halted. The closest forward (10) still pinned the opposing central defender, blocking any attempted wider cover. However, with the run beyond starting much higher, the defensive midfielder (7) was tracked better by the opposition's central midfield, and thus this occurred less than the underlapping wide centre-back.

The closest forward (10) would also make runs across, receiving from the wide wing-back (2). Although this was often covered by the first central defender, the wing-back (2) or closest defensive midfielder (7) then exploited the inside channel, targeting the gap now emerging between the opponent's two centre-backs. Although this resulted in another setting pass back, slightly delaying the ball into the penalty area, Brighton maintained their frequent progressions forward and numerous runners attacking through the gaps of the opposing back line.

When using a back five, the opposition had a stronger covering presence behind their widest defender, so both the run forward and the pattern of Brighton's wide build prior had to be adapted. Their wide centre-back (4) still predominantly provided the run beyond, but now as an overlapping movement instead, with inside dribbles from the wing-back (2) instigating the movement. The wing-back (2) either played reverse passes beyond to combine directly with their overlapping team-mate or, when direct access was covered, they utilised the two inside channel supports

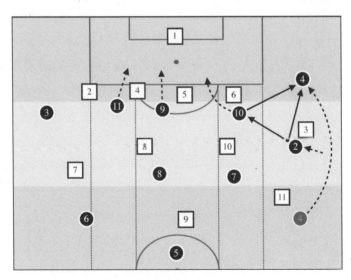

(7, 10) to find the overlapping wide centre-back via a third-man combination.

Although the wide forward (10) frequently tried to spin inside and attack the first space between the opposing central defenders after such a combination, runs in behind weren't always possible. If the combination occurred much closer towards the touchline, or the subsequent cross from the wide centre-back (4) was delivered first-time, the closest forward (10) then held off as a cut-back option instead, reducing the number of runs in behind. In these moments, the farthest wing-back (3) once again added a third run into the penalty area where possible.

Alternatively, the combination was made via the closest defensive midfielder (7), usually when the receiving wing-back (2) wasn't as high up the pitch. The closest forward (10) could then add their own penalty area run between the opponent's back line, not needed in the initial wide area combination. This also opened up rotations between the front trio – ideal if the best aerial threat started at the near post, for example, but needed to move further away from the ball before it was delivered across.

Should the diagonal dribble continue well into the inside channel then Brighton's closest defensive midfielder (7) performed the overlapping run through the wide areas, as the wide centre-back (4) re-established the double pivot.

From here, the only third-man combination for the wing-back (2) was via the closest forward (10), where Brighton would again only have two main runners attacking the cross, unless the far wing-back (3) joined in at the far post.

Opposing wing-backs eventually grew wary of these wider rotations as the season progressed, then prioritising tracking Brighton's overlapping runs instead.

The opposing central midfield then came across to press the wing-backs (2) from the inside, with the back line also shifting across to cover Brighton's through balls, within the inside channel.

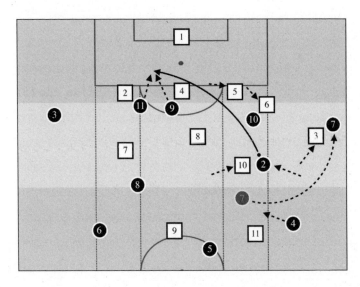

But from this defensive shift, the first two opposing centre-backs were bypassed by lofted deliveries towards the far post, targeting Brighton's two farthest forwards (9, 11). Any time the opposing back line failed to begin in a side-on stance, Brighton's front line had the edge, with their runs matching the flight of the cross. The far wing-back (3) attacked deeper deliveries placed beyond the opposition's wing-back, working the ball back across goal for the front line to finish. Whenever Brighton utilised two central forwards, and one attacking midfielder in the front line, this strategy proved particularly effective.

When facing a much deeper and more compact defensive block, Brighton maintained their patient attacking approach. It has to be said that their counterattacking exploits were fairly irregular over the 2020/21 season, often choosing to build and create through sustained possession after regaining possession instead of quickly progressing forward. One notable strategy from Brighton's back-three structure revealed itself once possession was settled, the wider centre-backs driving forward with the ball, luring out opposing pressers.

As Brighton's double pivot once again rearranged, the defensive midfielder (8) pushed into a more central position, with the closest forward (11) now moving wider. This strategy was seen most when Potter selected two attacking midfielders to support a single central forward as the initial front trio.

During the drive out from the back, the wide centre-back (6) often targeted the opposing winger, with the wing-back (3) patiently offering a pass around, positioned towards the touchline. Should the opposing winger press inward, blocking this pass, then the wide centre-back (6) utilised his central team-mates (8, 11) to either bounce the ball outward towards the wing-back (3), or inwards towards the front line (9). Whenever the opposing wide midfielder pressed outwards from a narrow starting position, access into the wing-back (3) was open.

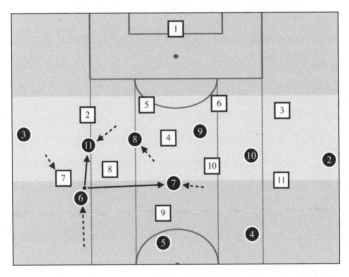

This dribble forward inadvertently created a double pivot – albeit offset – for Brighton, as when the opposing second line was particularly compact and well staggered in front of the ball, play was quickly switched across towards the more conservative defensive midfielder (7) to exploit gaps through the other inside channel, or wide area.

Yet disguised passes from the wide centre-backs also helped to break the opposing second line, both into the wing-back (3), and the inside-forward (11). By facing a particular team-mate, the wing-back (3) for example, the closest opponent would eventually read this body shape, and assume to predict the direction of the pass. From here, the closest opponent then began to move across, ready for a potential interception, but often overcompensating before the ball was actually released. The next closest defender frequently failed to match this quicker sideways movement, creating a bigger gap between the two for Brighton to exploit.

With a gap now open, the timing of the release from Brighton's wide centre-backs was crucial. When cutting the ball back inside while still facing the wing-back, the perfect moment to release came as the first opponent was balanced on their inside foot while moving out towards the wide area. This made it almost impossible for the opponent to instinctively react and change direction back the opposite way, and intercept the pass reversed past their inside shoulder.

This technique was also used when Brighton passed into their wing-backs, as the wide centre-back now faced inside first, narrowing the opposing second line. The opponent once again overcompensated their positioning, but now moving inwards. Brighton's wide centre-backs then reversed the ball out towards the wide area, now most effective when the first defender was balanced on their outside foot, again unable to shift their momentum in time for the pass around.

Brighton also managed to pull opponents out of shape via wider rotations involving the front line, now swapping with the wing-backs. Through Potter's use of two central forwards and just one attacking midfielder, the front line dislodged the opponent's full-backs after moving wide, before dropping towards the ball within the wide areas.

Brighton varied this strategy across the season, sometimes using it exclusively on one side of the pitch, and on other occasions performing the movements through both wide areas simultaneously.

Although this furthered their progressions beyond the opposing second line, when both central forwards were wide and deep Brighton's front line was then comprised of an attacking midfielder, and their two wing-backs. Resulting chances at goal naturally posed less of a threat, contributing slightly towards their inability to take the opportunities they created. But when Brighton used this rotation through one side of the pitch only, keeping at least one central forward around the opposing centre-backs, their penalty area threat improved while not reducing the quality of delivery.

The timing of this rotation confused opposing full-backs more than anything as they took over marking Brighton's central forward (11), once they'd moved wide. The trigger for the wing-back (3) to burst forward came as the now wide forward (11) dropped, dragging the full-back along with them. The attacking midfielder (10) and other central forward (9) then pinned the opposing central defence, prohibiting cover and further enhancing this wide gap.

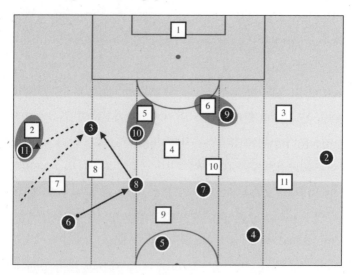

Brighton's double pivot (7, 8) and back trio (4, 5, 6) superbly recognised when to build between themselves, allowing the first initiating movements to occur. A pass forward too early, and the wing-back (3) wouldn't have moved into position in time, whereas a pass too late would see the opposition's back line – and closest full-back especially – reposition and cover the gaps. Therefore, through the quality and understanding of when to penetrate forward, Brighton's deeper units matched the timing of their rotation wonderfully, with penetrative forward passes setting the fluid front line on their way.

When using this rotation against a deeper block, Brighton's wide central forwards (11) were able to cut inside and shoot across goal, now using the wing-back runs as decoys. The attacking midfielder (10) also ensured they moved away from the ball, furthering the inside channel space available for the wide centre-forward (11) to cut inside and shoot. From a systems perspective, this didn't change Brighton's overall structure. But this particular rotation did create new gaps to penetrate, usually when their other wider strategies hadn't yet created chances.

Along with all the above rotations, patterns, and movements, a simple receive and push down the line before crossing from Brighton's wing-backs also created a considerable amount of chances for the front line. When no team-mates were needed to combine in the wider areas, and the wing-backs could deliver by themselves, Brighton had their maximum threat moving forward to attack the space in, and just outside, the penalty area. Whether through complex rotations, or simple yet direct drives forward, Brighton's creative threat across the 2020/21 season had variety, creativity, and quality, and was only missing consistent conversion.

4

Finishing

Premier League 2020/21

The total number of shots attempted in 2020/21 was lower than any of the five campaigns prior, but the percentage of shots on target continued its trend of increasing year on year since 2016, finishing at 39.9 per cent for 2020/21. Shots hitting either the post or crossbar were also at a six-year high, despite the overall reduction in attempts on to goal.

The total number of crosses was at a six-year low, as was the total number of entries into the attacking third, and penalty area. Although the total number of counter-attacks was also the lowest it's been for six seasons, the number of shots stemming from counter-attacking moments was at its highest since 2017.

As anticipated from the above data, the overall number of attacks through 2020/21 was lower than any seen from the five years prior. However, the number of central attacks was marginally up on the 2019/20 season.

A total of 1,024 goals were scored across 2020/21, the second-lowest figure for a single Premier League campaign since 2016, and 19 goals below the average across the five previous years. Some 760 goals were scored from open play, with 130 scored via the first or second phase of a set piece. A further 32 own goals were scored across the season.

A total of 102 penalties were converted out of 125 taken, with the second-highest success rate of the five seasons prior. However, that 125 was comfortably the most awarded across the same period, potentially due to the growing influence of VAR on the game.

Specifically through 2020/21, 653 goals were scored inside the penalty area, with the 107 remaining open-play efforts stemming from outside of the box. Fifty-one per cent of these 653 scored inside the area were converted from the space between the six-yard box and the penalty spot, sometimes known as the 'second six-yard box', proving a particularly key area through 2020/21.

Fifty-eight per cent of all open-play goals were scored first-time, with a further 20 per cent converted from a player's second touch. There were 91 open-play headers, with 660 finishes via the foot, and the remaining nine attributed to any other body part, predominantly deflected efforts. Sixty-one per cent of open-play shots or volleys were scored via the right foot, with 39 per cent from the left.

Arsenal

Mikel Arteta lead Arsenal to eighth for the second year in a row, with Bukayo Saka's goal away at Southampton the only effort from their 41 open-play goals to be scored from outside the penalty area. Inside the area there was a relatively even split regarding the positioning of the finish, with 13 goals inside or in line with the six-yard box, 15 ahead of the penalty spot, and 12 coming from behind it. However, over half of these were scored first-time, with the detail and quality of assist crucial, particularly after inside channel build-up.

Arteta ensured that either his winger or full-back held maximum width at all times, then performed horizontal runs across the back line before receiving a straight pass through the inside channel. This created a more natural running angle onto the ball, allowing earlier crosses, cut-backs, or passes back inside. Quicker deliveries then benefited the finishers, who could perform first-time efforts on to goal, without the need to reposition, or take additional touches.

When the gap to pass through was covered, central dribbles from the attacking midfielder (10) or centre-forward lured opponents narrow to then connect into the wider threats. Dribbles in front of the back line also exposed opposing full-backs, especially when Arsenal's joint second-highest scorers in the league, Pierre-Emerick Aubameyang and Nicolas Pépé, (7, 11), started to move inside before the full-back had begun to decelerate, catching them off balance, and less likely to dispossess the dribble inside.

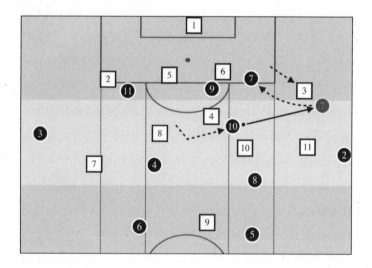

Aston Villa

Dean Smith led Aston Villa to an impressive 11th place in 2020/21, scoring more goals than any side in the bottom half of the table. Along with their improved defensive performances, Villa secured their highest finish since 2011, with the joint-youngest squad based on total minutes played.

Villa deployed the most left-sided attacks in the division, totalling at 1,231, 89 ahead of Manchester United in second. For comparison, Smith's side weren't in the top ten for right or central attacks on goal as they worked the most shots in the league from the left.

Despite missing 12 games, Jack Grealish's (11) ability to carry the ball into the penalty area – the league's highest – dominated this side, dragging multiple opponents along with him. Matt Targett (3) then overlapped from full-back, providing a strong crossing threat from early deliveries, especially benefiting from the smoothness and accuracy of Grealish's releases.

Centre-forward Ollie Watkins (9) frequently drifted on to the right centre-back, further aiding Grealish's dribbles, while also offering his own finishing threat from wide play. Delayed forward runs from Ross Barkley (10) or John McGinn (8) provided a secondary threat around the other central defender(s) whenever Watkins couldn't move across.

As Grealish finished the season in a more central role, El Ghazi was used on the left, providing an additional finishing threat – scoring four goals in the last seven games of the season – as a more central Grealish and Watkins occupied the majority of the back line.

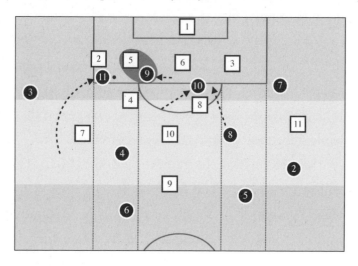

Brighton & Hove Albion

As we saw in the last chapter, Graham Potter guided Brighton & Hove Albion to 16th position, equalling their best Premier League points tally of 41 which had been set the year prior in Potter's first season in charge. Incidentally, they also had the third most shots blocked in the league, with 138 efforts covered by an outfield opponent.

Eighty per cent of Brighton's open-play goals were scored via right-footed efforts, with a particular emphasis on finishes within the second six-yard box. There was a relative split between right, central, and left-sided attacks, however, the right certainly provided much more assists.

Brighton's crossing was generally more accurate from their right. This was enhanced further by the supporting runs from the right side of their central midfield pair, or delayed assistance via the right-sided centre-back. Ben White (5) was outstanding in this regard, especially compared to Adam Webster who provided identical support but as a right-footer attacking from left centre-back.

However, as Brighton's narrow front trio was also heavily influential in Potter's attacking play, further link-up work with inside-running wing-backs, or dropping forwards, supported their right side especially. Pascal Groß (2) also proved particularly influential in his varying roles across the season, with his team-leading eight assists all coming from the right.

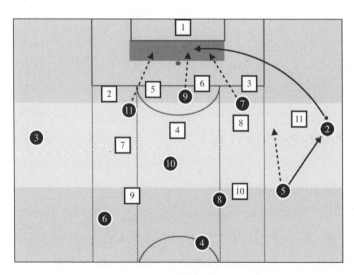

Burnley

Sean Dyche secured another season of Premier League football for Burnley, despite the team registering their lowest total of league goals for the past five seasons. The 2020/21 season also ended with Burnley's lowest Premier League finish since promotion in 2016.

The second-oldest squad used through 2020/21 heavily relied on Chris Wood, who was the only player to score more than four times, responsible for 36 per cent of all Burnley's league goals. As can be expected via their 4-4-2 structure, access into the two central forwards (9, 10) was frequent and direct. The timing of one run beyond to slightly stretch the opposing centre-backs, with another dropping short to receive the forward pass, was well demonstrated across the season.

Wood predominantly dropped to secure the pass in, with Jay Rodriguez, Ashley Barnes, or Matěj Vydra then being available to move the ball on to. But with the run in behind also performed across goal, opposing centre-backs were split and dragged simultaneously, allowing more room for Wood in particular to secure the pass in the first instance.

Wider access into the penalty area also proved important for Burnley, with the left-sided duo of Charlie Taylor (3) and Dwight McNeil (11) providing over 100 crosses each, as two left-footers attacking around the outside of the opponent's block. Right-footed right-back Matt Lowton (2) was next highest on Burnley's crossing list, but Dyche's right side often lacked a second right-footer ahead of Lowton, with many of their assists from the right coming from slightly deeper positions.

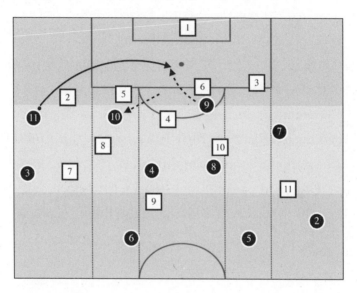

Crystal Palace

Roy Hodgson took Crystal Palace to 14th with the oldest playing squad in the league. Ninety per cent of Palace's open-play goals came from inside the penalty area, with their wingers key in both the creating and finishing of chances. Hodgson began the season in a 4-4-2, with Wilfried Zaha as a second central forward,

Andros Townsend on the right and Eberechi Eze on the left. Hodgson then utilised a 4-3-3 with Zaha and Townsend as wingers, and Eze in an attacking midfield position.

Palace relied heavily on inside dribbles from the left, and direct crossing from the right. Townsend (7) delivered the most crosses for Palace, almost twice as many as Zaha in second, targeting central forward Christian Benteke (9). Eze (10) and Zaha (11) then performed the most dribbles, coupled with quick combinations to help Palace progress, as they were extremely reliant on their left with the third most attacks in the league from this side of the pitch.

Disguised passing from Palace's left helped break into the penalty area, with impressive timing of release

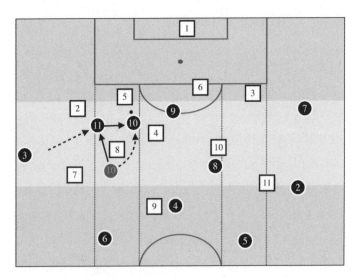

proving particularly effective. Both Eze and Zaha frequently changed their speed as they carried the ball through the inside-left channel. As the pair rolled the ball between both feet, they patiently waited until their opponent committed into a lunge, before breaking through via progressive passes and runs off the ball for return passes.

Chelsea

Thomas Tuchel took over from Frank Lampard midway through the season, guiding them to fourth on the final day. From his 19 Premier League matches across 2020/21, Tuchel averaged two points per game but with a relatively low-scoring return of 25.

Midfielder Jorginho ended as Chelsea's top scorer in the league, despite the club spending considerably on Timo Werner, Hakim Ziyech and Kai Havertz, who, as a trio, had scored 46 league goals the season prior for their respective clubs, but instead returned just 12 in their debut Premier League campaign.

Almost 95 per cent of Chelsea's open-play goals were scored inside the penalty area, with 71 per cent scored with first-time finishes. But specifically under Tuchel, the majority of Chelsea's assists involved sideways or backwards passes, often stemming from both inside channels, where forward runs from the narrow front line connected with very direct passing, especially as their double pivot remained very deep, staying close to Tuchel's back three.

The wing-backs then provided width to build around the outside of an opponent's press, as well as providing direct forward passing along the touchline, with Chelsea's main attacking trio still very high and closely connected. When facing a deeper block, Chelsea again exploited the inside channels with the two inside-forwards making frequent, underlapping runs to receive and create, with the second six-yard box responsible for almost half of Chelsea's open-play goals.

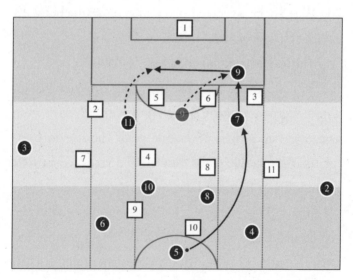

Everton

Carlo Ancelotti secured a tenth-place finish with Everton despite a strong start to the campaign, sitting in second after 15 games. They were among the leaders in the league for the percentage of open-play goals scored first-time, with lots of service from both the wide areas, and inside channels.

From Ancelotti's 4-3-3 James Rodríguez (7) pushed inside from the right, allowing Séamus Coleman (2) to overlap. But as Lucas Digne (3) provided similar runs from left-back, his closest partner in Richarlison (10) drifted higher when moving inwards, becoming a secondary central forward threat alongside Dominic Calvert-Lewin (9). The central midfield trio then covered for these individual movements, while also providing service through the inside channel, and additional forward runs through similar spaces, especially when Richarlison was high and Rodríguez even more central.

Ancelotti then utilised a more defined central forward pairing, predominantly in a 4-4-2 but also via a 3-5-2 on occasions. The wider combinations then increased in importance as Everton still focused on creating direct deliveries into the penalty area, and closer passes into one of the central midfielders as they ran through the inside channels. This then saw Calvert-Lewin and Richarlison both find success inside the six-yard box, with nine out of the duo's 14 open-play goals scored here

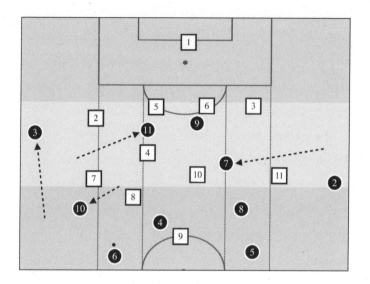

Fulham

Scott Parker couldn't save Fulham from relegation in their return to the top flight as his side scored just 27 goals, the second fewest in the division and lowest from any side in the last four years that didn't finish bottom of the table.

Although Fulham would attack using similar movements on both sides, their right returned the majority of assists through both the inside channel and wide area. From Parker's 3-4-3 structure, the width was provided by the wing-back, with the inside-forward very high but keeping the centre-forward through the middle, ready to attack between the opposing centre-backs. The closest central midfielder also moved across into the inside channel, with the wide centre-back then pushing in line with the midfield pair, enabling the wing-back to create further depth and runs in behind.

Fulham's right side then possessed more attacking threat individually, and collectively, as Ola Aina (4) – who has predominantly played much further forward in his career prior – provided aggressive runs as the right-sided centre-half in the trio. Wing-back Bobby Reid (2) was also converted from a higher threat, with the inside-forwards of Ruben Loftus-Cheek, Ademola Lookman or Ivan Cavaleiro (7, 11) positioned high and between the lines, creating the most chances for Fulham across the season, usually, after build-up play on their right.

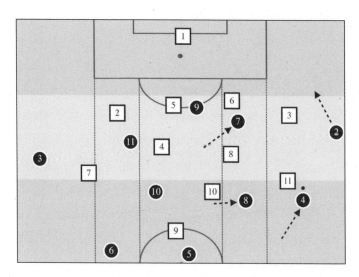

Leeds United

Marcelo Bielsa secured a ninth-placed finish in his first season in the Premier League as his Leeds United side registered the third-most shots on target across the division. They also had the biggest percentage of left-foot goals from open play, with top scorer Patrick Bamford accounting for almost half of these.

An impressive feature of Bielsa's side was the ability to cover ground and penetrate the penalty area with forward runs off the ball. From the 4-3-3 structure, the movements from the two wingers allowed Bamford (9) to hold a central position, ready to attack around the opposing central defence for much longer. Jack Harrison's (11) runs from the left were much more direct, often attacking on the outside of the full-back, whereas Raphinha (7) on the right would move inside much more, both with and without the ball.

Attacking midfielders Rodrigo, Mateusz Klich, Stuart Dallas or Tyler Roberts (8, 10) also performed frequent runs forward, predominantly penetrating through the inside channels. Further, slightly delayed, support from full-backs Luke Ayling (2) and Ezgjan Alioski (3) ensured Leeds could place anywhere up to five consistent runners working towards the penalty area at any one time.

Bielsa's lesser-used 3-3-1-3 saw a second central run alongside Bamford, with Harrison and Raphinha reprising their winger roles. Two inside-channel runs were then provided from Leeds' second line, often as full-backs moving inside, especially whenever the two wingers held the width.

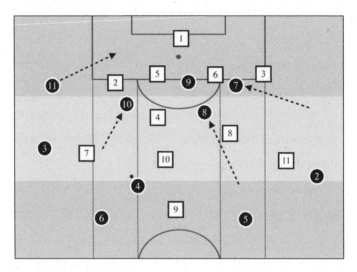

Leicester City

Brendan Rodgers led Leicester City to their first FA Cup victory in 2020/21 but failed to secure a place in the top four, as they lost out on the final day to finish fifth for a second consecutive season. Despite scoring 55 per cent of their open-play goals first-time, they also registered the highest percentage of goals scored from three touches or more.

Rodgers used a wide variety of structures across the season, with their assists predominantly sourced from the three most central lanes and few from the wide areas.

From the back-three structures, the presence of Jamie Vardy (9) and Kelechi Iheanacho (11) offered simultaneous threats in behind as well as the ability to secure the play around the final third. With accurate forward passing from the back line, or deeper midfielders, Leicester progressed the ball into these runs before connecting into inward movements from the wing-back (2) or the central midfielder (10), but usually those opposite to the initial forward pass.

Vardy impressively worked the inside-left channel, especially when paired with another permanent central

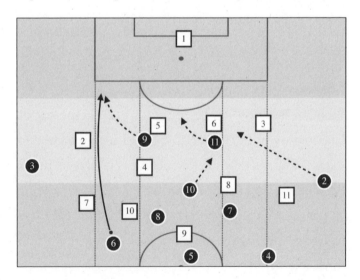

forward. This also proved a key transitional outlet for Leicester and although he finished as their top scorer in the league, Vardy also finished with the most assists, with almost all of these coming after cutting diagonally into the penalty area before sliding the ball across goal for right-sided finishes.

Liverpool

Jürgen Klopp failed to retain the title with Liverpool but managed to secure Champions League football for another season as his side finished in third place, some 30 points fewer than their title-winning campaign.

Sadio Mané and Mo Salah were again responsible for just under 50 per cent of all Liverpool's Premier League goals, despite registering their lowest combined return as a pairing. Diogo Jota added another central link either in place of, or alongside, Roberto Firmino. The dropping movements to receive away from the opposing back line meant both Salah and Mané had the room to move inside, and attack as Liverpool's highest goal threat.

Full-backs Trent Alexander-Arnold and Andy Robertson provided quality attacking deliveries across the season, with an often unappreciated skill of delivering the pass with enough bend to find the stronger foot of Mané or Salah. Thiago Alcântara's arrival also provided Liverpool with more centrally splitting passes, connecting further into the narrow front line, dropping forwards, or advancing full-backs. Although Thiago may not have provided goals and assists directly, his ability to manage the ball under pressure while still creating forward progressions helped Liverpool deliver their highest number of passes while under Klopp, as well as their highest average duration of each ball possession.

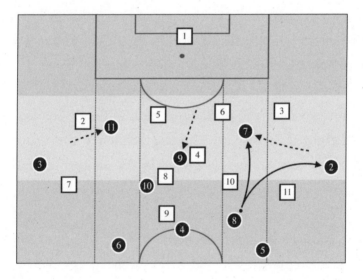

Manchester City

Pep Guardiola won his third Premier League title in four seasons, yet his team's 83 goals was the lowest tally for any title-winning side since Leicester City back in 2016.

Central midfielder İlkay Gündoğan registered their most in the Premier League, with Manchester City often deploying no recognised striker across the campaign.

Seventy-one per cent of the assists came via the inside channels, as narrow runs from a variety of players persistently exploited the gaps between the opposing full-back and centre-back. With no recognised striker (9), multiple rotations between a host of players made it very difficult for centre-backs and defensive midfielders to recognise who to mark, and which players' runs to prioritise tracking.

Just under half of City's goals through 2020/21 came from the second six-yard box, often via the second runner, finishing low passes across the penalty area, or cut-back crosses delivered right on the verge of the byline.

Maximum width from the wingers (7, 11) targeted beyond the opposing full-back, with City's own full-back (3) often moving into a central position to protect against opposing counter-attacks while also pushing one of the midfielders further forward (10). Ideal, then, to create the second central runner to help finish off attacking moves. Although City didn't rely on one player to score a significant proportion of their goals, no team managed as many different players to score more than seven league goals across the season as their six.

Manchester United

Ole Gunnar Solskjær led Manchester United to their highest finish under his tenure, and their best in the Premier League since 2018. United had the highest percentage of shots on target across the 2020/21 campaign, with 56 goals scored from open play.

The assists from their left tended to be deeper than from the right as Marcus Rashford (11) would move inside from the left much earlier than Mason Greenwood or Daniel James (7). Aaron Wan-Bissaka (2), although moving forward from right-back, crossed almost half as much as Luke Shaw (3) across the season. But to account for the slight shortfall, Bruno Fernandes

(10) would drift across from his attacking midfield role and provide extra deliveries. Due to his ability to receive away from pressure, and overall attacking influence, Fernandes would also cross from the left, usually moving in place of Rashford.

United had a significant finishing influence within the second six-yard box, with 67 per cent of their open-play goals coming from this particular space. Fernandes's mobility also helped place both wingers inside, with one often moving further inwards to become the main central forward. This allowed Edinson Cavani (9) especially to drift blindside of opposing centre-backs, before attacking deliveries into the penalty area, with outstanding individual movement across the face of goal.

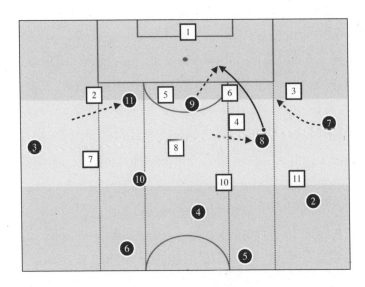

Newcastle United

Steve Bruce took Newcastle United to 12th, one place and one point higher than the season prior. Ninety-four per cent of their open-play goals came from inside the penalty area, with a central forward pairing key throughout the season for Bruce's side.

Newcastle were predominantly set up in either a 3-5-2 or 4-4-2, and were quick to access their two central forwards where possible. The wing-backs provided an immediate option to bend quick balls in behind or drive forward before crossing into the two forwards. With Newcastle often defending deep for lengthy periods prior to attacking, these wider outlets proved extremely useful to quickly access their front line, as did the deeper passing of Jonjo Shelvey.

In support of the forwards, central runs from the midfield contributed to Newcastle's goals across the season, especially as one of the adopted central forwards in Allan Saint-Maximin or Miguel Almirón (11) dropped short towards the ball. Joe Willock's (7) goals proved invaluable for Bruce's side, with delayed runs attacking crosses, cut-backs, and the second phase of any play directed towards the penalty area, with centre-forwards Joelinton, Callum Wilson, and Dwight Gayle (9) often occupying both centre-backs, before runs from midfielders such as Willock gave Bruce another attacking threat without losing balance and cover behind the ball.

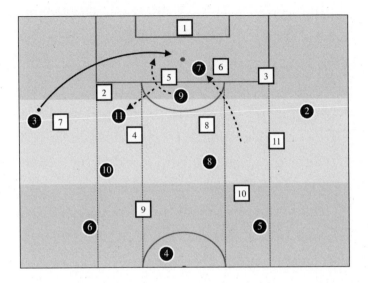

Sheffield United

Sheffield United failed to build on their impressive ninth-placed finish of 2019/20, ending the season bottom of the league with just 23 points. Their goals scored also fell significantly between the two seasons, dropping from 39 to 20, the lowest in the Premier League since 2008.

Interim coach Paul Heckingbottom took over from Chris Wilder with 11 games to go, maintaining the back-three structures which had proven successful in the seasons prior to 2020/21. The Blades continued to create most through the wider spaces, with multiple rotations and movements.

Top scorer David McGoldrick (9), who actually accounted for eight out of the 20 goals, continued to drop from the central forward pairing, particularly effective at linking between the wing-back (2) moving forward through the wide area and central midfielder (7) via the inside channel. Their other centre-forward (11) then kept a high position, primarily occupying the spaces between the opposing centre-backs.

Their own wide centre-backs (5) continued to push forward, especially prominent underlapping through the inside channels, as the single pivot (8) then covered underneath. The farthest central midfielder (10) would provide secondary support towards the high centre-

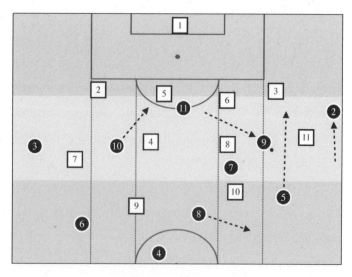

forward, with McGoldrick offering underneath the wide advances. With opponents focusing on the initial wide play, the centre-backs pushed on, with their direct opponent – often a centre-forward – regularly unwilling to recover back, especially when required to run back deep into their own defensive half.

Southampton

Ralph Hasenhüttl ended his second full season and third overall in 15th place, a drop compared to 11th the season prior. Hasenhüttl's side were second only to Manchester City regarding the most central attacks, as their 4-4-2 structure provided multiple narrow passing options.

Both wingers often positioned themselves inside, closely paired to the central forwards, who also looked to exploit the inside channels. Southampton then targeted the spaces between opposing full-backs and centre-backs upon their regains, with at least one, but usually both, of the two highest forwards eventually drifting between the centre-backs.

Southampton could then quickly attack after a regain without requiring complex changes and rotations. They began narrow as a pressing unit anyway, and could quickly launch forward with the front four supported by wider full-backs and two deeper central midfielders.

When finishing from a more patient attacking move, Che Adams would drop deeper – creating the most chances across the season – with Danny Ings remaining high but still moving on to the outer shoulder of the centre-backs, where he could finish from range or after running in behind from equal measure. As both wingers continued to narrow, one would replace Adams's higher starting role, with Theo Walcott and Nathan Redmond both key in this regard. Stuart Armstrong's central and wide roles in midfield also provided similar supporting movements, with Kyle Walker-Peters and the crossing play from Ryan Bertrand assisting further from the wide areas.

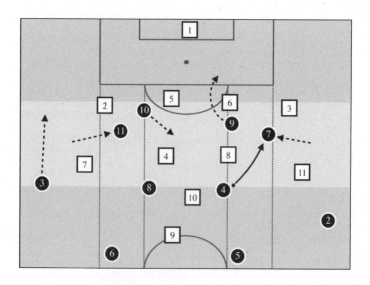

Tottenham Hotspur

José Mourinho was dismissed in April 2021, ending his 17-month reign, with Ryan Mason taking over for the remainder of the season. Spurs finished in seventh position, their lowest finish since 2009.

The relationship between Harry Kane, and Son Heung-min saw the pair assist each other for 14 goals across the season, a new Premier League record. Kane (9) dropping deeper as the central forward was the stand-out feature for Tottenham, with as many assists from the midfield third, as the final third. Three of Kane's 14 assists came from inside Tottenham's own half, with his range of forward passing superbly weighted for his winger team-mates, and Son (11) in particular, to run inside and expose beyond high full-backs.

Kane also demonstrated the ability to receive higher with his back to goal before turning on his first touch to enable early forward passes. He could hold off centre-backs who stepped out, as well as turn sideways to deliver an angled pass in behind, as a superb link between the lines.

Whenever Kane wasn't used in the build-up, or had enough time to return to a high position, his movement to the right was often found via Son's inside-left position, strengthened when Sergio Reguilón (3) overlapped from left-back and Pierre-Emile Højbjerg (4) covered from the double pivot in Tottenham's 4-2-3-1. Gareth Bale (7) also benefited from a similar inside-right position from Son's final ball, with valuable additional goals across the season.

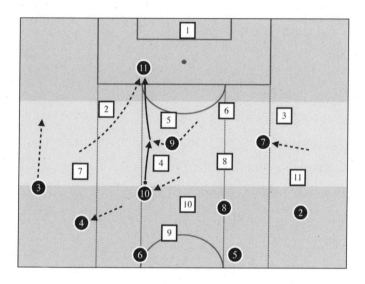

West Bromwich Albion

Sam Allardyce took over from Slaven Bilić in December 2020, but despite saving many teams in the past, Allardyce suffered his first relegation from the Premier League as West Brom finished second-bottom.

West Brom did score the most goals from all the bottom-four sides – 35 – with 25 coming from open play. From their 19 goals inside the 18-yard box, 53 per cent came from the spaces behind the penalty area as strikes from a relatively long range proved most effective.

Matheus Pereira (10) carried the strongest attacking influence as West Brom's leader for league assists through 2020/21. His dropping movements from a high, central position and weight of pass proved key in creating for the efforts beyond the penalty spot. Pereira would also showcase his own shooting qualities from this space, usually in the moments where he held his higher position.

Goals closer towards the six-yard box were clustered more towards West Brom's right, with full-backs Darnell Furlong (2) and Conor Townsend (3) as the two most regular crossers frequently aiming for this area. Pereira's narrower crossing, and forward passing in general, also

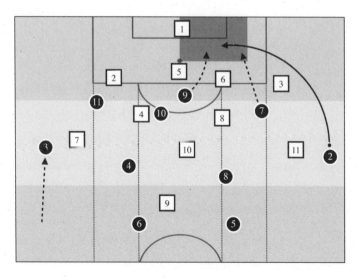

found this space as he dropped away from the penalty area, particularly when positioned more towards the inside channels, before providing diagonal passes from both sides of the pitch, aiming towards West Brom's effective finishing space close to goal but on their right.

West Ham United

David Moyes secured European football for West Ham United after a superb sixth-placed finish. Moyes's side posed a transitional threat, with the third-most counter-attacks across the season, while also being among the top sides for counter-attacks with a shots.

West Ham were also among the league's best for set-piece goals coming from either the first or second phase. But from more prolonged possession, Moyes's team often relied on the deliveries from Aaron Cresswell (3) and Vladimír Coufal (2), with the duo used in both wing-back and full-back capacities. Cresswell was also used as a left-sided centre-back, where his crossing came from a withdrawn position, accounting for his open-play assists coming well before the penalty area, with Coufal's inside, or alongside the opponent's box. Ninety-three per cent of West Ham's 46 open-play goals were scored inside the penalty area.

Central assists stemmed through West Ham's front line, with Jarrod Bowen (7), Michail Antonio (9), Jesse

Lingard (10), and Pablo Fornals (11) all contributing, and finding team-mates within the second six-yard box. Fifty-six per cent of all West Ham's open-play goals in the penalty area came from this particular space, with penetrative passing finding a central runner as the pass before the actual assist, often taking defenders away from the eventual goalscorer. A slight delay before this pass lured defenders towards the ball while providing time for a central team-mate to reposition, ready for the eventual effort on goal.

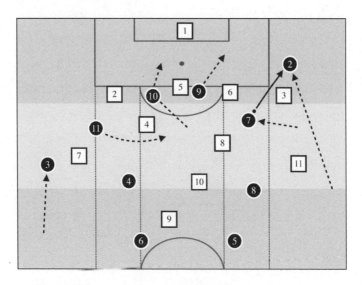

Wolverhampton Wanderers

Nuno Espírito Santo ended his fourth and final season as head coach of Wolverhampton Wanderers with the team in 13th, their lowest since promotion in 2018. They scored 36 goals in total, the second-lowest from the non-relegated sides, and 13 fewer than their league average across the two seasons prior.

A lengthy injury to Raúl Jiménez and the departure of Diogo Jota to Liverpool certainly contributed to the drop in goals as the pair had provided 47 per cent of all Premier League goals under Nuno prior to 2020/21.

Through 2020/21, Wolves scored 70 per cent of their open-play goals inside the second six-yard box with 62 per cent of open-play goals also scored with first-time efforts. They ranked lowest in the league for attacks on the left, but the third-highest for right-sided attacks with many of their goals were then coming from the right of the penalty area.

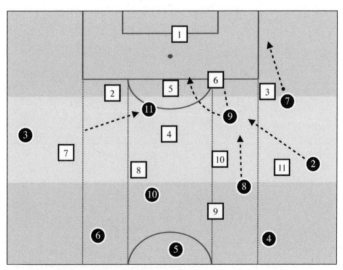

As Wolves progressed into the final third, they had numbers through the right inside channel as the full-back/wing-back narrowed (2). Wolves' left forward (11) then drifted into the central spaces, further adding to the close passing options as the ball progressed up their right side. The pace and direct running threat of Adama Traoré (7) burst around the outside of the opposing back line, with inside channel runs from Nélson Semedo, Daniel Podence and Pedro Neto providing the close combinations and sideways passing, for attempts inside the second six-yard box.

5

Attacking Transition

COUNTER-ATTACKING IS often associated with teams who directly attack the opposing goal in the immediate moments after regaining possession. But as the distance to goal is dependent on where on the pitch the ball is initially regained, how a team progresses forwards during this transitional moment will vary.

Some teams attack the opposing goal after intense counter-pressing, or defending high up the pitch, aiming to press and regain possession much closer towards the opposing goal. This transitional style is often associated with teams who also aim to dominate possession. They will then use intense counter-pressing, and/or higher defending to create further chances, and stop the opposition from creating periods of sustained possession, or counter-attacks of their own.

Counter-attacking, however, is more affiliated with teams who prefer to initially defend deeper, rarely regaining in the opposing half of the pitch. This deeper defending, although extending the distance toward the opposition's goal, increases the spaces available to attack after the regain. By beginning deeper, this allows the opposition to start and build much higher, naturally luring them away from their own goal. As long as the actions after a regain are then quick, forward, and performed with quality, counter-attacks can prove a particularly useful attacking strategy to win football matches.

Initially in the moments prior, counter-attacking allows teams to remain defensively solid and organised, and particularly difficult to break down. As some opponents then push more players forward with the aim to break through this deepened block, further spaces appear for quick counter-attacks. With football such a low-scoring sport, one or two successful counter-attacks per game can often be more than enough to claim a positive result.

David Moyes took over West Ham United for a second time in December 2019 and secured their top-flight status via a 16th place finish. Moving through 2020/21, Moyes's side impressed across the season and despite not quite matching their record Premier League finish of fifth they still managed to end up ahead of London rivals Tottenham Hotspur and Arsenal to claim sixth spot and European football for 2021/22.

A core aspect to West Ham's 2020/21 season was their ability to counter-attack, and create attempts at goal using this particular strategy. Moyes's side created the third-most counter-attacks across the entire division, often utilising three of four players to push forward from their defensive block. Although they only kept 11 clean sheets – the 13th best – only one side outside the top four scored more goals than they did, as they could also create from longer spells with the ball as well as having a constant threat from set-piece moments.

West Ham would also sit off prior to their counter-attacks, naturally encouraging the opponents further forward. As a result, only five of the non-relegated sides had fewer regains in the opposing half than Moyes's side across 2020/21, with a disciplined block the prerequisite for West Ham's attacking play.

Principles

West Ham primarily counter-attacked with three players responsible for the bulk of the attacking work. But depending on both the initial structure in the defensive phase, and the personnel used, the attacks were performed via slightly differing movements.

With West Ham utilising three main players ahead of a deeper fourth – often providing the initial forward pass to initiate the counter – the opposition were constantly reacting to the direction and choice of pass. Counter-attacking with just two main runners naturally provides fewer passing options, thus making it more obvious where and how the attack could develop. Three players also helped fill the central lane, and both inside channels simultaneously, allowing West Ham to attack in all relevant directions and further adding to their unpredictability.

In order to truly affect the opposing last line, the positioning of the attacking trio was also important, especially as they moved forward. Occupying spaces far enough away from the ball helped create possible gaps within the defence while still remaining close enough to support, distract, and combine when required.

Yet when too close to one another, opposing defenders could simultaneously deal with the ball carrier and the supporting runner with one simple body adjustment. This would heavily delay the counter-attack, allowing further players to recover and press from behind, likely to add to an already overloaded situation in the opponent's favour.

Managing these distances when moving forward also meant West Ham's runners acted as the first delay around the ball, should they lose possession at any point during the counter-attack. This also allowed those team-mates further back to begin the reorganisation into a new defensive phase. This strength in numbers and overall balance behind the forward running trio was superbly managed by Moyes, not turning matches into end-to-end contests but instead securing impressive results through patient, organised, and controlled spells of defending, before waiting for their moment to explosively penetrate via the counter-attack.

No matter how West Ham actually worked the ball forward, engaging the opposing centre-backs as early as possible proved key. Whether that was running beyond, directly dribbling at them, or rotating between, putting them under pressure as quickly as possible began the shift in momentum away from the opponent's attacking phase. With this in mind it also meant that any recovering opponents had a greater distance to recover, as in theory, the quicker West Ham affected the centre-backs the bigger distance the opposing second line had to work back.

During West Ham's progress forward, another consistent theme throughout was the change of direction via the two supporting runners, adapting their movements around the player carrying the ball forward. By not running in straight lines, West Ham's runners made it difficult for opposing defenders to track these movements while also keeping the ball within their eye line. The act of weaving, dropping shoulders and moving into new spaces, all while running at a very high speed, enabled West Ham's attackers to lose their marker and move into positions away from pressure.

These angled runs also helped the player on the ball to penetrate deeper into the opponent's half by using these movements as decoys and distractions. Fake releases combined with an overlapping or underlapping movement manipulated the opposing back line to prepare for a pass. By diverting attention towards the spaces away from the ball, opponents instead prioritised tracking the movements. The ball carrier not only gained more ground from this, but also avoided any recovering opponent pressing from behind. These runs also allowed the ball carrier to move into a more effective shooting position, as long as they maintained balance and control of the drive forward. January arrival Jesse Lingard best showcased this during his goal away at Wolverhampton Wanderers, carrying the ball forward for an impressive 52 metres as Michail Antonio ran across the pitch, dragging his marker inside, allowing Lingard to penetrate and finish.

Straight-line runs did have their place though, usually when West Ham utilised a more direct counter-attack via one long pass in behind. This more direct pass played predominantly over the opponent's last line created a straightforward foot race between West Ham's single central forward and the corresponding defender. Here, the detail of the pass changed to aggressively bend inwards after the flight of the ball initially started outside the opposing centre-backs. This minimised the chances of an interception or a headed clearance while still placing the ball to finish centrally for West Ham's main runner. Any further support from additional runners was required as quickly as possible to catch up with the often isolated forward. Therefore, these runs were performed as efficiently as possible, and thus using much straighter movements.

If a set, or backwards, pass, was involved at any point of West Ham's counter-attack, then it was usually followed by a more direct forward pass, accounting for the lack of initial forward progress. This was most common when the opposing back line initially squeezed forward to aid pressing their own loss of possession, while also stopping West Ham's centre-forward or supporting players from turning forwards. Although the set or backwards pass was sometimes forced by the opponents, the act of squeezing up did provide West Ham with more space to hit in behind, where straighter runs again supported a direct, bending pass forward.

As Moyes often instructed one of his higher players to work back alongside the central midfield unit during the defensive phase anyway, West Ham regularly had enough numbers to regain the ball in the first instance before then targeting the remainder of their front line. A key aspect here was to focus play towards the attacker who had remained high, usually on the other side of the pitch. By skipping the closest passing options upon a particularly deep regain, West Ham could also avoid counter-pressing actions from the opposition, initiating the counter-attack into an area far away from opposing numbers.

In theory this also limited the potential for opposing recovery runners closing around West Ham's primary ball carrier, with a longer pass also requiring a longer recovery run.

When the supporting runs were used and shorter passes performed, they usually occurred in the moments where the defenders focused more on the ball carrier and let the runners go slightly. Initially it's very important that as much ground is made up as quickly as possible in the moments after the regain. So if a player can't pass, then driving up the pitch is the only forward alternative, as long as there are appropriate spaces to do so. But a change in touch from West Ham's ball carrier often helped entice defenders prior to the release into a team-mate.

Once the attack had progressed deep enough to nullify any threat from recovering opponents, or when reaching the opposition's last line, the ball carrier moved from large and few touches to small and frequent. After slowed slightly during these multiple touches, defenders were then enticed, allowing where quick releases via front-foot passing to exploit beyond or around the closest opponent.

Through West Ham's use of this particular passing technique, almost all defenders found it practically impossible to predict and anticipate the release, and thus block the pass. Opponents would have to be touch-tight to the ball carrier to cover this front-foot pass, leaving even more space for West Ham's runners to move into. Then coupled with the change of angle and position from the supporting runners, West Ham struck the balance extremely well of consistently gaining ground after the regain and then adapting to create quality chances.

This dribbling to attract soon became a key component, the longer West Ham's central runner stayed on the ball, especially while still covering ground, the more opponents were lured towards the ball. And just as with the bending runs of support, the ability to change lines during a dribble also displaced opponents by dragging them into different areas. Emerging spaces then opened for differing supporting runs, providing more opportunities for disguised releases via the front-foot passing technique.

The timing of the release itself was also well performed, especially when the closest opponent was off balance. But even when the defender was in control of their movements, and in a set jockeying position, West Ham still found ways of releasing into a team-mate. For the most part, they'd pick the exact moment when the opponent was partway through stepping towards the ball as the ball carrier then passed in the opposite direction, preventing the defender from decelerating, and blocking the ball.

Although this only made the defender take one or two extra steps as they slowed down to turn, and face the new West Ham player in possession, it created enough valuable seconds for the receiving runner to progress forward, and/or create a chance, especially when the ball was moved from the central lane, towards a runner moving through either of the two inside channels.

4-2-3-1

As expected, West Ham's centre-forward was always involved in their counter-attacking play in some way. When utilising four lines from the 4-2-3-1 in the defensive phase, it was common that the two wide midfielders provided the additional runs forward. It was therefore extremely rare that the central forward dropped back to secure possession, and three other runners moved ahead instead.

From here, the centre-forward (9) primarily drove through the central lane, with the two wide midfielders (7, 11) narrowing to move forward through the inside channels. Early releases then allowed the centre-forward to reposition off the ball, predominantly moving in behind, and attacking the spaces in front of goal much quicker.

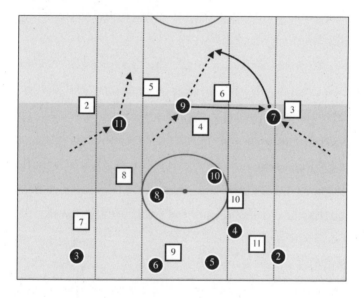

Crosses or through balls then bent inwards challenged many opposing central defences, turning them to face as much of their own goal as possible as the ball was delivered.

Whenever West Ham's far wide midfielder (11) made a second forward run attacking around the farthest defender, then the angle for a clearance away from goal was reduced further. This often resulted in tentative defending from the first defender, unable to clear across the pitch while still facing their own goal. This was enhanced further when West Ham's central forward released the ball early, as they had the most instinctive mindset to then attack the spaces in behind, whereas other runners held off on occasion.

Prior to the regain, it was common that one of West Ham's second line worked back and positioned themselves deeper. This was to support the two defensive midfielders, with Moyes's defensive blocks within their own half sometimes requiring additional central protection. This was most common when West Ham utilised a back four, enabling one of the double pivot to cover across the pitch, and assist the inside channels, and spaces ahead of the centre-back and full-back pairing. Naturally, then, this had a huge effect on the following counter-attacking phase, and especially which three primary players moved forward.

As already established, the central forward was consistent within West Ham's counter-attacks. So for the most part it tended to be the player who had worked back the most during the defensive phase, then sacrificed out of the main body of the counter-attack. The resulting movements, positioning, and method of breakaway then varied, as the three highest players quickly adapted to equally fill emerging spaces, before performing quick and incisive actions on the ball to progress up the pitch.

One example of this is an adaptation of the previous breakaway involving the central forward, and the two wide midfielders. Should one of the wide midfielders have dropped back alongside West Ham's double pivot then the counter-attack was formed via the central forward, number 10, and remaining wide midfielder, placed slightly higher on the other side of the pitch. Whenever the central forward drove through the middle of the pitch, the number 10 then adapted their movement to fill the inside channel vacated by the deeper wide midfielder. Once the new trio was established in the three central lanes then the principles of the previous section were performed to varying levels, depending on what was required, and, most importantly, how the opposition defended upon the change of possession.

As an alternative to West Ham's central forward (9) holding their position, they also made wider movements, often spinning off and working away from the opposing centre-backs. This helped exploit the spaces left by particularly adventurous full-backs, who were often lured further forward in the first instance due to the depth of West Ham's defensive structure. In these moments the centre-forward's (9) run was often matched by a more direct forward pass, played over the opposing pressure. With the supporting runners then required to catch up with this more direct forward play as quickly as possible, it was often the number 10 and far wide midfielder (11) who performed the straight and efficient forward runs. And because West Ham's centre-forward had moved to exploit the wide space, the wide midfielder (7) on that same side was often much deeper anyway, tracking the runs of the opposing full-back, who'd already moved forward quite significantly.

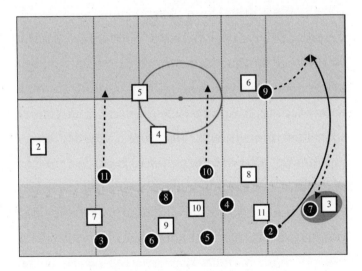

A widening run from the centre-forward was also used when West Ham drove forward with the ball, allowing a wider ball-carrying midfielder, for example, to cut inside and into the central lane. From here, either the number 10 moved over towards the other inside channel or, if the number 10 was involved in the deeper regain, then the other wide midfielder would continue their support from their side, with fewer movements required. Once again the changing of angle here was superbly demonstrated by both the ball carrier, and the closest supporting runner. And when paired together, the simultaneous changing of lanes and position was especially hard for opponents to track.

A widening central-forward run also made space for a deeper drive from West Ham's number 10, dragging players away from the main burst forward. But this movement also increased the effectiveness of any forward passing, now gaining ground through combinations, and attacking the increased central spaces for through balls. Here, the disguised releases and timing of forward passes were best showcased as West Ham's number 10 occupied the central lane, then finding passing targets towards both sides. Releases into a wide midfielder who carried a goal threat from an inside position, such as Jarrod Bowen, or the bending runs made by the central forward, Antonio, both resulted in particularly effective counter-attacking displays, with the number 10s Lingard or Pablo Fornals as the main passing threat.

5-4-1

With an additional player placed into the back line in the 5-4-1 structure, West Ham's defensive block changed slightly, no longer forming four distinct lines of defensive pressure. The two defensive midfielders also lacked the protection of the number 10 in front, so narrowed together, leaving more space towards the inside channel. As a result, Moyes often placed the far wide midfielder inside of the pitch when defending, and slightly deeper. The additional presence of two wing-backs – who defended slightly wider and could press out quicker than the full-backs within the back four, due to the additional central defender – also contributed to the narrowing of West Ham's wide midfielder, especially, when Moyes's side were out of possession for a considerable period.

The central forward continued as the predominant threat on the break, again often supported by the two wide midfielders. Without the use of a number 10 though, the positions used for counter-attacks became more obvious for opponents. And as a result, West Ham's runners had to perform more varied movements, rotations, and changes of angle off the ball as they progressed forward. This saw an increase of multiple movements within the same attack, where, for example, the centre-forward may move wide to allow the wide midfielder to cut inside with the ball. But as the play then progressed, the pair reverted back as they moved across one another, also combining with much quicker passing. In comparison to the previous counter-attacking methods from the 4-2-3-1, where variety regarding positioning was easier to establish, more movements and rotations were required when counter-attacking from the 5-4-1 block.

However, as the season progressed, and with the two defensive midfielders (8, 10) often in line with at least one, or sometimes both, of the wider midfielders (7, 11), West Ham's double pivot soon provided an alternate counter-attacking player. This was often seen via a delayed run forward where the initial breakaway lacked the pace and penetration of other counter-attacking strategies. But by utilising a third-man combination – where the set back lured opposing screeners forward, making space for the third, delayed runner – West Ham found a new alternative method to progress forward.

Tomáš Souček was superb in this regard, providing a sturdy defensive base before then joining forward with powerful central runs. This movement often occurred as the central forward (9) drifted wider, allowing Souček to penetrate into central spaces. Declan Rice offered similarly athletic runs forward but would rarely commit into the final third. He instead acted as a more passive third-man runner, taking possession under pressure to allow West Ham's wider midfielders (11) to reposition and move forward, before releasing the ball.

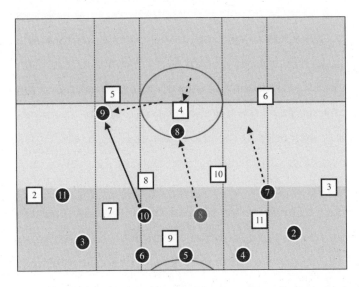

When regaining the ball from a mid-block, and closer to the halfway line, West Ham's 5-4-1 also provided wider counter-attacking opportunities through the wing-backs. There were brief moments where West Ham's midfield foursome all narrowed, and both wide midfielders were forced to defend deeper than they may have wished. But something unique to West Ham is that on their left especially, they had an additional crossing threat in Aaron Cresswell, who Moyes often converted into the third centre-back.

So when West Ham faced a side which also utilised a back five, and had more players behind the ball to deal with the threat of the counter-attack, their wider combinations created additional crossing moments as well as utilising the now narrow wide midfielders as extra support around the central forward. This was one of the rarer moments where West Ham utilised an extra player in the counter-attack, as the opposition posed less of a threat to counter the counter, with many players still deep prior to the initial regain.

5-3-2

One final structure used by Moyes placed an extra central forward in West Ham's first line, reducing the occupation and numbers within the midfield unit. Moyes would often use a double pivot behind an attacking midfielder, with the defensive block also beginning slightly deeper. With the wide areas more inviting for the opposition, this defensive depth encouraged forward runs from opposing full-backs, allowing West Ham to then target this area of the pitch as they regained possession. Due to Lingard and Bowen often leading the line as the central forward pairing for Moyes, bending runs from a central position proved the key outlet. The attacking midfielder then moved forward through the central lane, recreating the main trio and providing another team-mate between the opponent's centre-backs.

With the 5-3-2 placing two players in West Ham's first line, one of the central forwards (11) also worked back to press into midfield, increasing the defensive presence coming from behind the ball. This recovery then saw the slightly withdrawn attacker support outside of West Ham's second line, usually when the front line had attempted to receive wide, and were thus positioned much closer towards the touchline. This extra cover when defending focused around the outside of the defensive midfield pair, where the attacking midfielder (10) would also drop into the second line. In

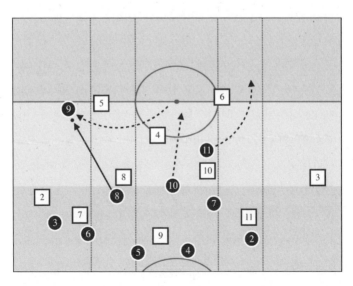

these moments, West Ham essentially adopted another variation of the 5-4-1 defensive block, before three main runners then moved forward upon the regain.

As the higher central forward (9) moved wide to receive the main breakaway pass from West Ham's slightly deeper block, central spaces were vacant for forward runs. As the number 10 pushed forward, the remaining central forward (11) then pushed wider to attack in behind and not close off the central space for the delayed run, especially if they worked back to support the defensive phase prior.

With Rice often absent from this particular structure, any defensive midfield runs fell solely to Souček, especially when the attacking midfielder – usually Fornals here – had covered deeper in the defensive phase prior. This run from Souček was also performed when one of Lingard or Bowen, as part of the central forward pairing, had recovered back to support the deeper defending. The attacking midfielder would then move outwards to free the central space for this second forward run from Souček.

Although West Ham then took slightly longer to rebalance their counter-attack, and affect as many opposing defenders as possible, the speed at which they progressed the ball forward often accounted for this, especially with both Lingard and Bowen ideal runners when working around the outside, and into the significant spaces left in behind from the opponent's back line.

6

Defensive Transition

THE MOMENT when a side loses possession, and the ball remains in play, is often known as the defensive transition. It is the opening period where a team no longer has possession of the ball and the priorities and roles of players begin to change. The timeframe in which this transition occurs differs in various coaching cultures and methodologies, and is also dependent on the objective of the transition.

Some teams take an assertive approach to losing possession, and look to place immediate pressure on to the opposing ball carrier and their surrounding team-mates. This is commonly known as counter-pressing. Alternatively, many sides try to delay the opposition by blocking and screening forward options, allowing their team-mates to recover into their primary defensive roles. This second strategy then enables the outfield players to create a prolonged defensive structure, moving into a less physically demanding, organised defensive block.

The art of winning the ball back quickly after its initial changing of hands is often associated with sides who look to dominate possession of the ball. Teams then prefer to defend by having the ball for extensive periods, limiting the amount of opposing attacks, and territory they can gain. Counter-pressing can also be used as an offensive strategy, as in the moment where the opposition regains possession many of their players will look to move into new spaces to help build an attack of their own. During this expansion, successful counter-pressing not only regains the ball but also helps take advantage of new gaps and spaces which didn't exist in the moments prior.

Creating quick counter-attacks is often seen as a way of beating sides who dominate possession, especially against teams whose players rotate and move far away from what could be considered their primary defensive role – some full-backs for example. So effective counter-pressing can also help deal with this particular attacking strategy, by prohibiting the opposition from working the ball forwards, and exploiting the spaces, and/or positioning of a possession-based side.

But what is also key for any side which hopes to be effective during the defensive transition is its structure with the ball, and in the moments prior to defending. Striking that elusive balance whereby players are positioned close enough in possession to create enough immediate pressure on to the ball when it is lost, but positioned far enough away from one another to create an effective attack in the first place, is the challenge.

Liverpool finished the 2020/21 Premier League season in third place, which was a disappointing return considering their two superb seasons prior, notably the title-winning campaign of 2019/20. When joining Liverpool in 2015, Jürgen Klopp brought with him an intense counter-pressing strategy which focused on creating chances by quick regains, creating the opportunity to exploit the opponent's conversion into a more expansive structure. However, as time has progressed, and Liverpool have adapted their strategies to dominate more areas of the game, so too has their defensive transition changed its priorities.

Through 2020/21, Liverpool regained the most loose balls across the season, with their overall ball recoveries the third-highest in the division. The only method of regain at which Liverpool were among the lowest was through interceptions, an understandable outcome as they often locked opponents into a deep defensive block through their build-up, leaving the opposition few passing options as they regained possession. This results in panicked moments on the ball, facing the repeated counter-pressing intensity; only Chelsea and Manchester City only had fewer interceptions than Liverpool across 2020/21.

With Liverpool also dominating more of the ball, and for longer periods, their counter-pressing has shifted towards pinning and protecting as opposed to creating and conquering. Liverpool now focus most on counter-pressing to stop opposing counter-attacks, and keep the opposition locked into a deep defensive block. Despite the slight change in objective, this strategy remains key for Klopp's side, and the famous intensity and aggression is still paramount.

Full-backs Forward

Anyone who has watched Liverpool from 2017/18 onwards will no doubt have seen how effective their full-backs (2, 3) have been. Trent Alexander-Arnold and Andy Robertson have provided unparalleled, simultaneous attacking returns, overlapping into positions high up the pitch. To create the room for these runs, Liverpool's wingers (7, 11) have naturally moved inside, also becoming the main goalscoring threat in the process. To further support these movements, the central forward (9) often drops slightly, both disrupting the opposing defensive midfielder(s) while also creating more room for Mo Salah and Sadio Mané as the wingers coming inside.

But to allow such aggressive runs from their full-backs, Liverpool need support around the ball, and then cover in the moments possession is lost. The midfield trio (4, 8, 10) mainly from a 4-3-3, but also a double pivot in the 4-2-3-1 structure, add vital protection underneath the ball. They are the key to covering the wide areas, especially when opponents try to counter-attack through their wingers, or wide forwards. Their positioning also enables forward pressing should the ball drop somewhere in the central areas, as well as providing secondary support to Liverpool's central defence (5, 6) when facing direct long balls, or less-thoughtful clearances from the opposition.

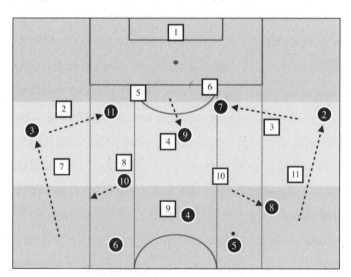

With Liverpool locking the opposition deep into their own half, the high centre-backs (5, 6) form the last outfield line underneath the ball. The sideways body shape from these two deepest outfielders especially allows them to push off and run back towards their own goal, or jump forward, and press further into the opposing half, in equal measure. But Liverpool naturally have to concede space somewhere on the pitch, and this is predominantly within their own defensive half, and is a consequence of locking the opposition so deep in the first place.

Liverpool have had various injuries within the central defence across 2020/21, and their high line has at times been susceptible during longer periods of defending. Yet this usually occurred when the front line was unable to pressure deeper central midfielders, who then picked more accurate passes in behind. For the most part, though, they remained in control during defensive transitions.

Depth provided by the defensive midfielder gave Liverpool's central defence further assistance in the central lane, able to receive headed knock-downs, or duel for the next phase if the ball remained uncontested. Further support arrived via the two central midfielders, now occupying much narrower positions. The ability of these two midfielders especially to move with the flight of the opponent's forward pass or clearance, but then appear closer than their direct opponent during the second phase, heavily contributed to Liverpool's frequency of regains, especially those that then ended up in an uncontested space.

It was also common for the defensive midfielder (4) to cover in between the centre-backs, with the wide areas also targeted via more calculated clearances from the opposition. Whenever these passes were hit particularly long, they bypassed Liverpool's covering central midfield (8, 10), proving more difficult to support the second phase. The closest centre-back (5) would then engage with the receiving forward or winger, as the defensive midfielder (4) then filled into the back line. The farthest central midfielder (10) then narrowed into the central spaces, covering for the defensive midfielder's dropping cover, with the closest central midfielder (8) often helping the engaged central defender to overload the receiving opponent, and account for any subsequent sets and lay-offs.

Against play that hadn't reached the areas around the halfway line, Liverpool's defensive midfield then had further licence to jump forward and apply more aggressive forward pressure. In keeping with Liverpool's impressive abilities to apply pressure quicker than many of their opponents, any slight increase of distance for

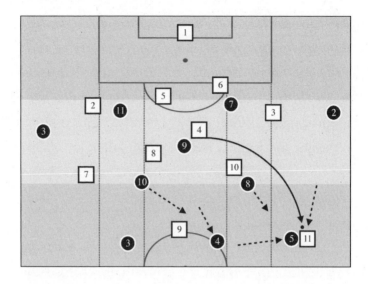

this player to cover rarely affected the team's defensive transition.

As the defensive midfielder (4) jumped, they usually did so primarily to delay the opposing counter-attack, unless there was a particularly high chance of regaining possession – a clear and obvious loose ball, for example. This delaying and screening of forward passes frequently stopped opponents accessing their central forward, prohibiting a key link in many counter-attacking moves that begin from deep positions.

This delaying and screening also bought crucial seconds to allow team-mates to move into areas no longer focused on attacking and creating, but instead on recovering and defending. With Liverpool usually performing significant positional changes and movements within their attacking build-up – especially during a lengthy spell of possession – reforming their preferred defensive block took significant energy and time. The full-backs were the best example of this, with a considerable distance to cover from an initial position of height and width, often beginning right up against the opposing back line, to then recover and to defend alongside their own centre-backs, and in the spaces behind if needed.

Therefore, this delaying via Liverpool's defensive midfielder (4) through the central lane enabled the full-backs (2, 3) to work back at least level with the second line, and just ahead of the two centre-backs (5, 6). Liverpool's closest central midfielder (10) then performed half-and-half support underneath the jumping defensive midfielder (4), further covering central passes. This narrow position also covered any wide through balls, should the opposing winger begin ahead of Liverpool's full-back (3), while still remaining close enough to press their direct opponent if needed.

Liverpool's farthest central midfielder (8) would initially offer more cautious support as the defensive midfielder (4) advanced. However, once the threat of an immediate counter-attack was nullified, and especially once Liverpool's corresponding full-back (2) had recovered into Liverpool's second line, they increased their forward pressure, now moving forward with the intent to engage the ball if it hadn't already been regained.

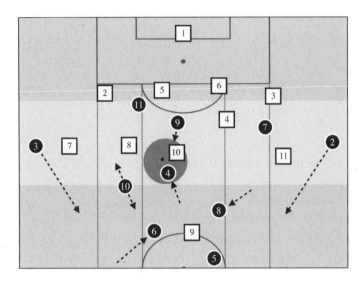

If the ball was played in the air, and the defensive midfielder (4) maintained their jump forward, then the central midfielders' (8, 10) positioning also provided cover in the rare moments the timing of press was misjudged, or the defensive midfielder (4) simply lost their individual duel a flick on for example. This also saved either of the central defence (5, 6) from stepping out too much, maintaining the overload around the opposing centre-forward.

Another core aspect of Liverpool's successful defensive transitions was the secondary pressure, most often applied as the forwards recovered back. With the front trio often staggered as the wingers inverted, this secondary pressure primarily came from the central forward (9) who had already dropped deep. When contesting central balls, Liverpool's central forward (9) helped the defensive midfielder (4) double-press both the space and the direct opponent, creating simultaneous pressure from multiple angles.

This additional, blindside pressure harassed the opposing ball carrier if they secured the ball ahead of a Liverpool player, often forcing a misplaced pass, or another on-the-ball error. Depending on the effects of this double press from Liverpool's front line, their deeper central midfielder sometimes readjusted their role, especially if it was unlikely that the opposition would regain possession, let alone counter-attack forward.

As Liverpool's front line pressure continued, the central midfielders converted into a screening role, blocking alternate passing options. Although they still maintained the aggression and reactions needed to jump on to any further loose balls when needed, Liverpool's central midfield pair focused on covering sideways passes out towards the wide areas. With Liverpool's front line often rotating between themselves as they created attacks, it wasn't uncommon for one of the wingers – now acting as the deepest, and central of the front line trio – to apply similar recovery pressure.

With Liverpool's full-backs both high, and frequently ahead of the ball, a secondary press from behind the ball also came through the wider spaces. As the pair worked back into Liverpool's second line anyway, Liverpool's full-backs turned this recovery run into a blindside press. In these moments, the closest central midfielder came across as the primary cover, with the defensive midfielder closely attached. The farthest central midfielder then temporarily filled in just ahead of the central defence, with Liverpool's full-back on the far side performing a much narrower recovery run.

Although the double-press strategy was most commonly showcased by the central forward, or the high full-backs working back, Liverpool showed further examples of this in all areas of the pitch as it became a particular theme throughout the season. When they lost possession through a misplaced or intercepted pass, the double press came from the player performing the pass and the attempted receiver. With Liverpool initially spacing themselves as far away from one another as possible, but as close as needed to maintain possession, these two players were best placed to deploy instant counter-pressure in most areas. The double press would alter for inaccurate passes over longer distances, however – a switch of play for example, – now seeing the closest players pressing the point of interception, which wasn't necessarily either the passer or receiver.

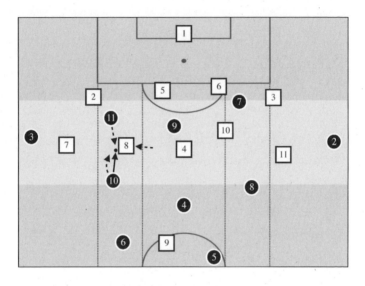

For passes played through short and medium distance, the role of the second presser would alter, depending on the direction of pass. During forward passes, the player waiting to receive applied secondary pressure from behind, as they were initially ahead of the ball when it was turned over. A pass from Liverpool's central midfielder (10) towards their winger (11), for example, saw the winger (11) press from behind, and the the central midfielder (10) closed off the spaces ahead of the ball while screening forward passing options. The

Elland Road welcomed Premier League football for the first time since May 2004.

Luke Ayling and Stuart Dallas were instrumental in Leeds United's build-up play.

Head coach Graham Potter addresses his players in the absence of Brighton's home supporters.

Leandro Trossard and Neal Maupay created the most chances for Brighton across the season.

Tottenham Hotspur forward Harry Kane receiving the Golden Boot, and Playmaker award for his 23 goals, and 14 assists.

Golden Boot winner 2020/21

Playmaker winner 2020/21

David Moyes celebrates leading West Ham United to European football for the 2021/22 season.

Captain Jordan Henderson, filling in at centre-back, organises his team-mates.

Liverpool boss Jürgen Klopp gives instructions to Mo Salah whilst visiting The Emirates Stadium.

Spanish midfielder Rodri regained the most balls in the opponent's half for Manchester City.

Two of the greatest tactical innovators in the modern game: Marcelo Bielsa and Pep Guardiola.

Dean Smith receiving a red card from referee Jonathan Moss, during a miserable evening in Manchester.

Aston Villa and England defender Tyrone Mings organising a defensive wall.

Tottenham's first choice double pivot Pierre-Emile Højbjerg & Moussa Sissoko battling for possession.

José Mourinho watches on from the sideline, against one of his former sides.

secondary pressure from behind had the sole intention of directly engaging the opposing ball carrier, whereas the player screening ahead of the ball was there to delay, as well as directly engage when possible.

Backwards passes played towards Liverpool's own goal would then see the roles reversed, for the most part. If the example pass was flipped, and the pass from Liverpool's winger (11) was intercepted en route back towards the central midfielder (10), then it became the passer who provided the more aggressive pressing first. The secondary press then comes from what would have been the receiving central midfielder (10) as they again screened and covered spaces around the ball, prohibiting the opposition from immediately progressing forward.

Because Liverpool are now so instinctive under Klopp, they often regain possession through this double-pressing strategy, usually as they've forced the opponent into a mistake of their own. It was very common through 2020/21 to see multiple Liverpool players pressing a single – and often isolated – opponent, and that has been paramount for Liverpool's pressing success under Klopp since his arrival.

Liverpool's front line also performed frequent higher counter-pressure, rushing on to the opposing back line and goalkeeper. This was predominantly to force early passes and prohibit deeper build-up as opposed to regaining the ball high through high pressing – although, they have still proved very good at the latter across Klopp's tenure.

As Liverpool's front line, or members of the trio jumped forward, often pressing underloaded, the two centre-backs condensed together with the defensive midfielder beginning their dropping movements in anticipation of a longer pass. Reading the cues and body position of the opponent on the ball played a huge part in the depth of this dropping from the defensive midfielder. A bigger first touch, a lay-off pass, a lengthy and aggressive stride towards the ball, or expanded arms and body shape all indicated that a particularly lengthy pass was incoming.

Liverpool's quick reactions from their deepest three players to change position and set their own body shape ready for the ball over helped them best prepare for direct play. Quick scanning from the two central midfielders ahead acknowledged the potential spaces for second balls, knock-downs, or instinctive clearances as a result of the aggressive pressure from Liverpool's front line, as well as how best to cover for the advanced full-backs if they were yet to work back. Because Liverpool often set up in preparation for the defensive transition much quicker than many opponents could convert into an attacking transition structure, the ball often ended up as a free collection for Liverpool.

In the often chaotic moments where the opposition attempted to counter-attack, Liverpool's central midfielders were also very effective at changing their opponent, and moving into a new area to engage with an alternate opponent. When the front line (7, 9, 11) didn't manage to force a long pass, or clearance into an ineffective space, the central midfield pair (8, 10) would support forward and take up higher positions. They did so in the quickest route possible, not particularly focused on forcing the ball specific ways, or moving on to specific shoulders of individuals. The aim here was to engage the opposing ball carrier, and choke the immediate spaces around the ball.

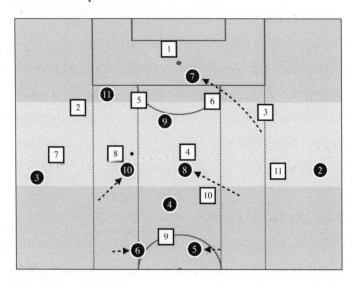

But as they jumped forward, the gap between the midfield and recovering players, and their back line grew slightly. So if the front line were unsuccessful at regaining quickly, opponents found a brief escape route before the second wave arrived. However, as the ball travelled, the central midfield (8, 10) again showed their worth by recovering back as the ball moved forward. For the most part, Liverpool's second line were quicker than their direct opponents, able to support the next phase of play, almost acting as the secondary pressure seen elsewhere.

It is also worth noting that should the opponent have progressed towards the halfway line, by this point both of Liverpool's full-backs had also worked back towards, and often beyond, their second line. And with the central midfield otherwise initially engaged with the opposing ball carrier, the full-backs then narrowed and condensed around the defensive midfielder. This accounted for the increased space ahead of Liverpool's last line, with plenty of bodies then ready to collect free regains forced by the pressing second line, albeit less quickly than seen in previous methods.

Full-backs Reserved

A significant amount of the progressive play that comes through the full-backs is also achieved from a more reserved position. This means that when the ball is lost, they are already part of the second line, and thus aren't required to perform the lengthy recovery seen when positioned high. This naturally gives Liverpool a much stronger immediate presence when their defensive transition begins, especially if only the front line have initially threatened high up the pitch.

For the most part, the full-backs will then press inwards when more reserved in the attacking phase, primarily supporting around the defensive midfielder. This gives more licence for the central midfielders to jump forward and aggressively counter-press along with the front line. And with the full-backs also reserved when attacking prior, the central midfielders may have already moved forward, ahead of or around the ball when it was lost. Therefore, the pressure from behind may also come more from the central midfielders, with the full-backs joining the defensive midfielder in screening forward options, and delaying the attack.

With the reserved full-backs (2, 3) also narrowed, it can give the central midfielders (8, 10) licence to press for longer, often then backed up by the deepest of the front line (9). Condensing around the opposing central midfield often sees Liverpool totally covering the three most central lanes, with the wide areas the only real escape for the opposition.

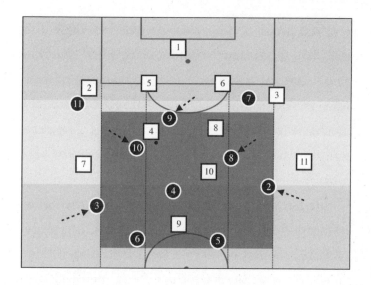

If the ball forward didn't match the timing of a wide forward run, the centre-backs (5, 6) quickly slid across, and collected the ball with relative ease. The cover between the two centre-backs (5, 6) was again performed by the defensive midfielder (4), where then one of the full-backs (2, 3) filled in centrally, as the central midfield pairing were now engaged sightly higher. However, against a particularly strong threat in behind, the full-backs also offered support inside of a widening centre-back, especially if the opposition continuously tried to counter-attack through one of the wider areas.

In these moments, the farthest full-back narrowed to support around the defensive midfielder, just as the central midfielder would do when they were covering for the full-back advances. It was essential for Liverpool that they maintained cover during their attacking phase, as even with their aggressive pressing numbers, sometimes due to the quality of the opposition, they would still get played through on occasion. Therefore, a strong and adaptable second line cover enabled Liverpool to contain counter-attacks, and maintain most elements of their preferred attacking shape prior.

With the wingers still looking to attack inside, even without the support of the full-backs around, they would often drag the opposing full-back inside with them. With all Premier League opponents fully aware of the qualities and goal threats Liverpool's wingers carried, the front line were well supported in counter-pressing via the more advanced central midfield pairing. This also allowed Liverpool to harry the opposing defensive midfielders, often forcing them to play passes, and release the ball much earlier than they might have wanted. With the second line then in place, Liverpool again secured possession through frequent loose ball collections.

But due to the growing fluidity of Liverpool's attacking play, especially involving moves of much longer duration, and an increased sequence of passes, they frequently combined one full-back high with one central midfielder forward. Many of their resulting attacks were no longer symmetrical, with both full-backs, or both central midfielders joining the front line trio.

So in these moments, many of Liverpool's strategies during the loss of possession were still maintained, with one of the full-back and central midfield pairing covering for the other. Only in the rare moments where they needed a late goal or were chasing a game did they forgo second-line cover. And as this was only in the rarest of moments across the season, usually towards the end of a match where the opposition was utilising a particularly deep defensive block anyway, Liverpool could adapt their second-line numbers, but only for brief moments.

On some occasions when facing two central forwards, Liverpool would push one full-back forward and place the corresponding central midfield cover further inside. This narrower position helped the defensive midfielder cover any access into the opponent's front line, while allowing for instant pressure on to the opposing midfield unit. Due to the qualities Liverpool possessed between the lines, the opponents in two units of four would stay very compact anyway, limiting the eventual support they could provide should they access their two central forwards.

They could then maintain a clear, and useful overload against the front line, with the more reserved full-back, and usually defensive midfielder, supporting the second phase as the centre-backs engaged with the opposing central forwards. The dropping cover in between the centre-backs would no longer be provided by the full-back, with either the defensive midfielder, or deepest central midfielder now covering into the back line instead.

Back Three

In response to some defensive structures, Liverpool would also form a very brief and temporary back three during build-up, often with the defensive midfielder dropping in between, or alongside, the two centre-backs. Here, both full-backs pushed forward once more, as their centre-forward continued to drop deep, allowing the wingers to invert. However, the central forward often dropped more exclusively to one side, as the central midfield pair then performed alternate roles.

Should the central forward move into the inside-right channel for example, then their left central midfielder would move up, connecting with the advancing full-back, and narrow winger on that side. The central forward then provided identical support with the other winger and full-back pairing, as Liverpool now committed more players forward.

With this increase in attacking options higher up the pitch, Liverpool's central, secondary pressure came from two players, with the advanced central midfielder (10) and dropping centre-forward (9) now both pressing from behind. The farthest (10) of these two away from the ball would also consider a screening role as they narrowed upon a loss of possession, prohibiting the opposing central midfield unit from combining, and potentially switching the play away from the central pressure.

This would also help to keep the ball in that compact central area where Liverpool are so strong at choking the play, and regaining through direct duels, or forcing mistakes into free regains. The closest (9) of this particular pair prioritised energy, pressing, and directly engaging on to the ball, and the direct opponent if necessary.

The two widest of the converted back trio (4, 6) then resembled further screening ahead of the ball seen prior, with the middle player (5) within Liverpool's back line dealing with central aerial balls, as well as direct clearances over.

Again, an adaptable body shape was key here, quickly recognising the triggers of when to approach and defend side one, for the step up short, or sprint in behind.

The two widest players (4, 6) in the converted back line also covered clearances and passes out towards the wide areas, with the deeper central midfielder (8) then dropping to cover within the temporary gaps growing in Liverpool's back line. As the wider spaces looked more tempting for the opposition to target against this particular Liverpool structure, the decision of jumping towards the ball or dropping back from Liverpool's two widest, temporary defenders (4, 6) was extremely important.

With such a defensive overload created by the back three against a single centre-forward, however, there was naturally more opportunity for, and onus on, the two wider members of the converted back line to step in and engage further, now moving alongside the deeper central midfielder (8). Should one jump forward, then a clear overload still existed around the opposing centre-

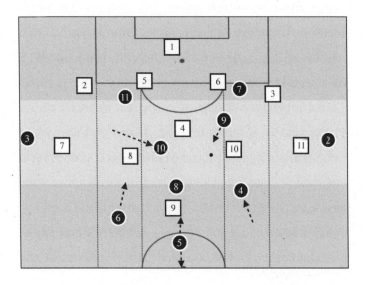

forward, something not necessarily true in the previous structure.

But where and how the transition was forming would also impact the decision-making of the two widest defenders (4, 6).

The closest would engage forward when contesting a higher loose ball, often courtesy of the extra, secondary pressure provided by the two central attackers (9, 10).

Whenever the closest opposing winger was particularly deep – possibly tracking the runs of Liverpool's high full-backs – the wider counter-attacking threat was minimised, also allowing Liverpool's wider defender to jump forward. In these moments, opposing counter-attacks only became accessible through the centre-forward running into the wide areas, where Liverpool's middle defender (5) could track and contest for the ball, with one of the two closest team-mates (4, 8), then filling in as central cover.

As Liverpool would also form a back three via one of their full-backs (2), the corresponding winger (7) would then hold the width, with the central forward (9) and opposite central midfielder (10) again forming a central pair, through each of the inside channels. With one of Liverpool's full-backs (2) now more reserved, and remaining a part of the back trio, Liverpool no longer needed their defensive midfielder (4) to drop. Therefore, Liverpool then had extra central protection ahead of the converted back trio, usually when the opposition left an extra player high, either as a high number 10, or as two permanent central forwards.

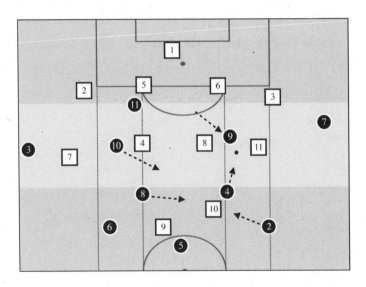

From here, Liverpool could always commit pressure in front of the ball from this second line, usually via the closest player to the ball (4). With aggressive secondary pressure then coming from the closest of the two higher central attackers (9), Liverpool's other central players narrowed towards the spaces around the ball, again stopping quick combinations, and the possibility of an opposing switch of play.

This narrowing from the supporting central players (8, 10) also helped to cover access into the feet of the opposing front line, with the closest full-back also tightening on to their opponent (2). This maintained a close overload, and allowed for subsequent pressure from multiple angles, should the opponent bypass Liverpool's second-line pressure, or attempt to play directly into the spaces in behind.

7

High Pressing

DEFENDING HIGH up the pitch focuses on two main principles. A team can apply high *pressing*, hoping to regain possession, ideally within the final third. Or, higher *pressure* disrupts shorter build-up play, forcing the opponents into unwanted, longer passes.

Yet higher defending isn't always possible as some sides immediately clear the ball out of their defensive third via any means necessary. Goalkeepers who kick all their set pieces long also neutralise any potential higher defending.

Pep Guardiola's Manchester City side has been meticulously studied, particularly his attacking play and control of the three most central lanes. His 4-3-3 structure often provides a key overload in these areas, especially when playing against a central midfield pairing, such as a 4-4-2 for example. Yet when up against a central midfield trio, his side often creates a four vs. three via the central forward dropping, centre-backs stepping forward or, most commonly, a full-back moving inside.

Aggressively pressing the opposition immediately when the ball is lost helps Guardiola's side gain further control by decreasing the time defending, and limiting how effectively the opponent can transition into attack. With Barcelona, his team focused on intercepting passes en route between opponents, with many of his pressers between two opponents in half-and-half positions, able to react and press multiple, potential passes.

The pressing personnel in midfield changed from the likes of Xavi, Pedro, David Villa, Lionel Messi, and Andrés Iniesta, to the much more combative Thomas Müller, Bastian Schweinsteiger, Arturo Vidal and Frank Ribéry as Guardiola then joined Bayern Munich. Here his counter-pressing focused more on duelling, and regaining through individual challenges in a man-for-man approach. City's pressing has been a blend of the two.

There is a clear insistence on controlling all play through the central areas of the pitch, likely stemming from Guardiola's own playing career as a pivot under the guidance of Johan Cruyff. This also applies to when defending higher up the pitch, as City have demonstrated four principles through 2020/21, no matter the shape or structure of the opposition.

1. Limit access from the opponent's back line into central midfield, through screening players, and/or half-and-half positions
2. Ensure there is a central overload in their favour, or at worst, it's numerically even
3. The cover on specific shoulders in the second line, is just as crucial as the pressure or screening from the first line
4. Press aggressively into the wide areas from the second or third line, once the first line has forced the play around

vs. A Back Three and Single Pivot

In some instances, the effectiveness of City's higher defending was reduced against teams who started with a back four, but then converted mid-game into a trio. But ironically most teams using three permanent centre-backs such as Wolverhampton Wanderers, Newcastle, Sheffield United, and West Ham, all took a very direct approach to their own deeper build-up, thus playing over City's attempted higher defending.

When up against a permanent back three, accompanied by a single pivot, opponents formed a 3-5-

2 structure. City's wingers (7, 11) and centre-forward (9) then pressed the three centre-backs, with the wingers predominantly curving their press inwards, covering the pass around, and into the wing-backs. The central midfield trio then matched up man for man, forming their own double pivot (4, 8) behind a single advanced midfielder (10).

A common strategy by many teams – City especially – is to bounce the ball around a pressing opponent, often via a central midfielder in a third-man combination. So the nearest double pivot (8) covered the outer shoulder of their opponent, attempting to block the pass into the temporarily free wing-back. When the central forward (9) locked the play on to one side, City's highest midfielder (10) covered between the opponent's two

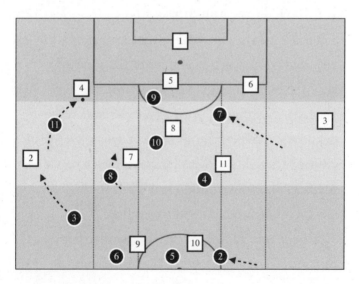

closest central midfielders, with the farthest winger (7) narrowing considerably, ready to join the press inside if necessary.

With the play locked on to one side, the closest full-back (3) moved forward, ready for an aggressive press on to the opponent's wing-back. As with the farthest winger (7), the remaining full-back (2) narrowed, creating a three vs. two overload against the central forward pairing.

When opponents avoided this higher pressing, they played directly into their front line, as City's defensive midfielder (4) then dropped deeper, no longer marking an opposing midfielder, but zonally covering the three inside lanes instead. To maintain a three vs. three in central midfield, the centre-forward (9) reduced their

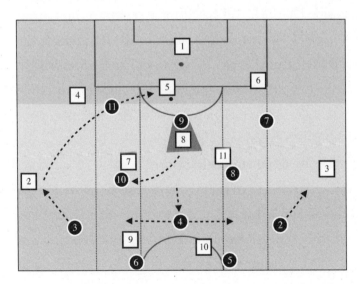

higher pressing on to the middle centre-back, instead screening access in front of the opponent's single pivot. The advanced midfielder (10) then dropped back in place of the now deeper defensive midfielder (4), reforming the double pivot.

With the long central pass covered, play was forced into the wide areas. The deeper three vs. two overload created by the dropping defensive midfielder (4) allowed City's full-backs (2, 3) to start much higher than before, considerably reducing the pressing distance towards the opposing wing-backs. The inward-pressing wingers (7, 11) then became the first line of defence, continuing their press on to the middle centre-back.

Any aggressive full-back press towards the wide area saw the defensive midfielder (4) cover across into the inside channel, still blocking access into the central forwards. When the wingers (7, 11) didn't press the middle centre-back, they worked back toward the receiving wing-back, double-pressing with the full-backs (2, 3).

vs. A Back Three and Double Pivot

When a back three was supported by a double pivot, opponents used a narrow front trio instead of the central forward pairing, thus forming a 3-4-3 structure. Whenever the middle centre-back possessed the ball, City's two attacking midfielders (8, 10) continued their cover on the outside shoulders of their opponents, ready to block a third-man pass toward the wing-back. But a slightly withdrawn half-and-half position was also needed, to cover the inside channels, and stop the centre-backs passing straight into the feet of the wide forwards. The central forward (9) would again force the play one way, doing their best to cover access into the feet of the double pivot, where possible.

City's wingers (7, 11) also took up a narrower starting position as their positioning had to be intelligently measured when the opponents had an extra player in the front line. Starting too narrow allowed the middle centre-back to pass around City's first two lines of pressure, playing directly from middle centre-back, out to the free wing-back. This is a strategy City actually use themselves, albeit from centre-back to winger. Yet when their winger (11) was positioned too wide, and too close to the wider centre-back, then a pass would split between the winger (11) and attacking midfielder (10), once again finding the feet of the wing-back and breaking the entire press.

When perfectly positioned, play was forced over the wingers' heads, where the full-back (3) aggressively covered into the wide area. The closest centre-back (6) then moved across as the back line converted into a temporary trio.

Basic human mechanics dictate that players move best when facing forward. So as the full-backs (2, 3) approached the ball head on, they gained maximum momentum into the wide area.

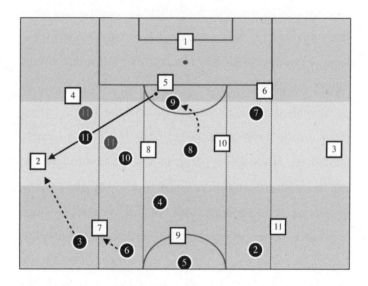

And as this particular pass was often delivered in the air – to avoid City's continuously aggressive first line – their full-backs were in a much stronger position to win the aerial duel.

Whenever the central forward (9) aggressively pressed towards the goalkeeper, and blocked access into the middle centre-back, the opposing double pivot usually dropped to assist the under-pressure goalkeeper. The central midfielders also took this as a trigger to follow, remaining tight on to their direct opponent.

Compared to outfielders, goalkeepers tend to make longer eye contact with the ball when receiving under intense pressure, therefore are more likely to miss passing options even if a team-mate close by has lost their marker.

When City committed to applying high pressure on to a goalkeeper, they did so with maximum energy and aggression, aiming to disrupt the build-up, as opposed to regaining possession high.

When the centre-forward (9) then forced the goalkeeper one way, the corresponding full-back moved forward earlier, ready to press towards the wide area. When pressing an aerial pass, the approaching full-back (3) still had a huge positional advantage over the opposition's wing-back. But should the full-back (3) lose the duel, the defensive midfielder (4) and closest defender (6) then overloaded the wider forward within the inside channel, dealing with any second balls.

vs. A Back Four and Single Pivot

From the 38 Premier League matches, City faced back-four structures on 26 occasions as many opponents then relied heavily on building through a single pivot. As a result, both wingers (7, 11) frequently became the two highest pressing players, blocking access between centre-back and full-back, with the central forward (9) slightly more reserved at times.

To apply pressure on to the goalkeeper, whenever the closest winger (7) moved on to the centre-back, the farthest winger (11) moved higher, and narrower. As the initial pressure naturally came from the same side as the ball, the goalkeeper's increased focus here left them blind to their opposite shoulder, where the farthest winger (11) could sneak in and press further. Alternatively, the original winger (7) continued their press on to the goalkeeper, pressing in the same direction as the pass back.

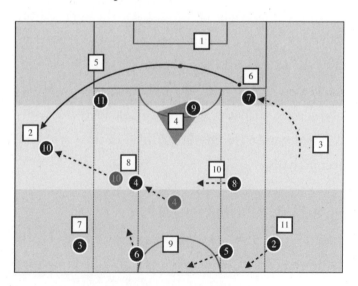

When a first-line regain wasn't possible, City's pressure once again forced the play into the wide areas, keeping the ball away from the pivot, and the central spaces in general. The central forward (9) screen nullified potential play into the pivot, with the central midfielders (8, 10) continuing to mark on the outside shoulders, prohibiting the third-man combination into the free full-backs.

As the passes into the wider area were over a considerable distance, and played in the air, it proved difficult for opponents to progress forward. Overhit, and the pass sailed straight into the empty stands. Underhit, and one of the winger (11) or attacking midfielder (10) would intercept. Even when perfectly flighted, the receiving full-back still found it difficult to control, due to the technique required, the touchline right up against them, and the aggressive pressure City immediately placed upon the wide areas. The variety of wide cover within this particular strategy best showcased both City's defensive qualities, and their adaptability across the 2020/21 season.

When up against lower full-backs, or should City want to maintain a plus-one overload within their back line, then the closest attacking midfielder (10) pressed into the wide area. City's four vs. three overload within central midfield allowed this particular press, as the defensive midfielder (4) moved from their zonal marking position in between, now on to an opponent. The farthest attacking midfielder (8) then covered inside of their man.

During this wider press, it was imperative that the attacking midfielder (10) didn't move underneath the ball, allowing the opponent's full-back to receive behind, and drive out. Therefore, winning this duel was crucial for the whole strategy. When under pressure, opposing full-backs would often try to progress the ball forward by any means necessary. And as the defensive midfielder (4) no longer covered the central spaces in front of the back line, City's centre-backs readied themselves for this potential next phase.

The closest centre-back (6) moved slightly in front of the opposing centre-forward, ready to jump on to a flick on from the full-back, whereas the farthest centre-back (5) moved into a side one stance, ready for a sprint back towards City's goal, if the play was hooked in behind. The farthest full-back (2) also took up a side-on stance, adding further cover in behind the centre-backs.

As the 2020/21 season progressed, some opponents who retained the single pivot narrowed their front line, encouraging the full-backs to move higher and beyond the line of the central midfielders (8, 10). Therefore, the full-backs would press into the wide areas instead, with better momentum gained compared to the central midfielder cover. The front trio (7, 9, and 11) performed the same roles as previous, as the defensive midfielder (4) began slightly deeper than before, adding further protection between the midfield, and defence, and keeping a deep overload.

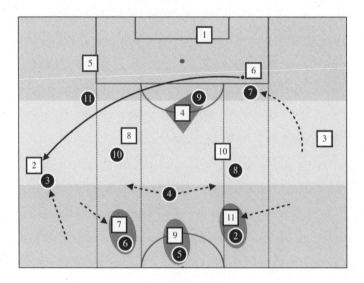

A 4-4-2 diamond structure also heavily relies heavily on building through the single pivot, while high fullbacks provide the width. With the central midfield presence increasing to four – instead of the three in the 4-3-3 system – the defensive midfielder (4) would then have their own player to mark, usually the opponent's highest attacking midfielder.

This meant if one of City's central midfielders pressed into the wide area, then the opponents had a free central player.

Therefore, the full-backs continued their aggressive jump out from the back when up against a midfield diamond as the back line again converted into a trio, zonally covering around and between the opponent's two central forwards, in a three vs. two. Although these two strategies with either the attacking midfielders (8, 10), or full-backs (2, 3) covering the wide areas predominantly occurred on both sides of the pitch, there were occasions when City mixed and matched the two ideas within the same fixture.

This stemmed from deeper opposing centre-backs increasing the pressing distance for City's wingers. When the opposition tried to find their now much lower full-back, it was the responsibility of the closest central midfielder (8) to cover the wide areas, with

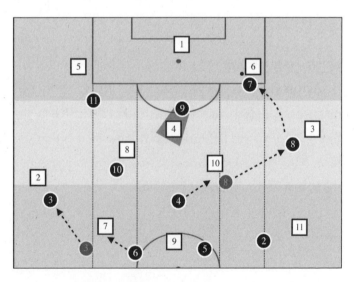

the defensive midfielder (4) taking over their original opponent, whereas against the high-moving full-back, the responsibility fell to the full-back (3), with the corresponding centre-back (6) moving across to mark the narrow winger.

This mix-and-match strategy was predominantly due to the pressing distance required. Speed of press is fundamental in any high-defending strategy, giving the opposing receiver as little time as possible to make a decision regarding their next action. City's central midfielders (8, 10) naturally started much higher than their full-back (2, 3) team-mates, allowing an earlier press high, and were thus better positioned to deal with a lower full-back. Their full-backs, meanwhile, had a stronger positional advantage to press against a higher full-back, compared to the sideways movements provided by the central midfield when they covered wide.

Across the season, City also varied the roles of both the pressing and screening within the first line. Whenever the central forward (9) aggressively pressed on to the closest centre-back instead of performing a screening role, they were joined by the farthest winger (11) who maintained their inward press. The centre-forward's (9) press then covered passes into the opponent's attacking midfielder through the inside channel, allowing the closest central midfielder (8) to move on to the opposing pivot. The closest winger (7) then retreated, covering on the outside shoulder of their new opponent, as well as the wider press towards a low full-back when needed.

On the opposite side of the pitch, the far central midfielder (10) maintained their role on the outer shoulder, supporting between the defensive midfielder (4) and high-pressing winger (11). The defensive midfielder (4) again blocked central play into the opponent's front line, as well as covering any wide press made by the more conservative winger (7), or the aggressive midfielder (10). This strategy was used when Guardiola selected a central midfielder player in one of the winger positions (7), and predominantly when the opponents kept their own wingers wide, and full-backs low.

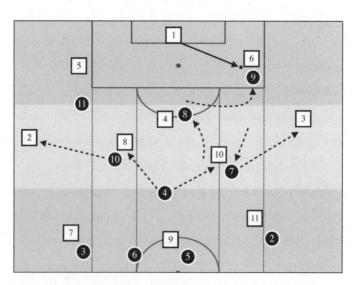

With the central forward now higher in the first line, City had a much quicker pressing influence on to the opposition's centre-backs, especially upon their first touch. This increased pressure on to the first moments of build-up and sometimes resulted in longer play into the front line, even if that wasn't the opponent's initial game plan. But when one of the opponent's full-backs pushed high, City's corresponding full-back again covered the wide areas, engaging alongside the deeper winger (7) or attacking midfielder (10). Because of this increase of early pressure by the central forward, the high opposing full-back usually came from the wide area opposite to the ball.

An alternate method saw the central forward (9) revert back to the screening role, with the front line now comprising the farthest winger (7) and the closest central midfielder (10) aggressively pressing from City's second line. As with the previous strategy, the cover into the wide areas came via the deeper winger (11), and remaining central midfielder (8).

The closest centre-back (6) readied to step forward, and deal with play into the front line in place of the defensive midfielder (4) who jumped to cover behind the aggressive central midfield (10) press. The farthest centre-back (5) then prioritised play beyond, as this strategy was best used when City had identified a particular weakness within one of the opposing full-backs, notably their reduced ability on the ball under higher pressure.

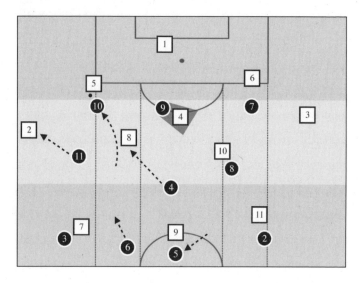

As City's attacking midfielder (10) pressed through the inside channel, they blocked direct passes into the feet of their original opponent. The defensive midfielder (4) then took over from behind, predominantly covering from the outside shoulder. But because play inside was screened, opponents were often funnelled into the free full-back, before City aggressively pressed into the wide area via their closest winger (11). Switches of play to the opposite full-back were then dealt with by the farthest attacking midfielder (8), and defensive midfielder (4) covering just behind.

City added further pressure into the wide area when needed via their full-backs. This helped double-press the opposing full-back, and accounted for forcing play into feet, as opposed to in the air. So although against this press the wider passes were easier to control for the opposing full-back, they often received the ball under much more pressure. Should the opposing full-back move beyond the covering winger (11) to receive an aerial pass, then City's full-back (3) would again take over pressing duties, with the back line going man for man once more.

vs. A Back Four and Double Pivot

When up against a double pivot and a back four, City often performed inward pressure on to the centre-backs via their wingers. But as the centre-forward now had a double pivot to block, they took up a half-and-half position between the two, primarily focused on stopping either of them from turning inwards. They also covered central access from the centre-back into the highest attacking midfielder, as opponents often formed a 4-2-3-1 structure.

City's closest central midfielder (10) also marked much tighter on the outside shoulder of their man, owing to the centre-forward's (9) inability to completely screen both of the double pivot. This outside-shoulder position also covered passes through the inside channel, in case the opponent's attacking midfielder or wingers tried receiving directly from a widening centre-back.

Unlike when against a single pivot, though, the centre-forward (9) had a secondary defensive responsibility, after the initial screening role. When the central midfielder (8) covered into the wide area, the defensive midfielder (4) was unable to cover across, already marking an opponent, similar to when up against a 4-4-2 diamond.

Therefore, to restore balance and order in the central areas, City's central forward (9) covered the central midfielder's (8) wide press, now marking their previous opponent. This strategy was used most when Guardiola selected a midfielder to play in the central forward

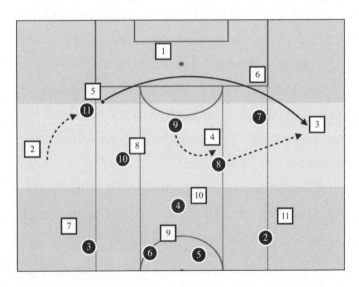

role, as the central midfielders (8, 10) continued their cover against lower full-backs. City's own full-backs (2, 3) would then deal with high opposing full-backs as seen before.

Some teams, often coupled with a more direct style, added another attacker around the defensive midfielder (4) – either one winger inverted, with the other moving high and now alongside the centre-forward, or more commonly, the central forward dropped away from City's central defence, with both wingers now high.

Either way, when up against a narrow 4-2-2-2 structure, City adapted their back line, while maintaining the winger's inward press, and central forward screen. Against the increase of direct play, the central midfielders (8, 10) covered the outside shoulders of their opponent,

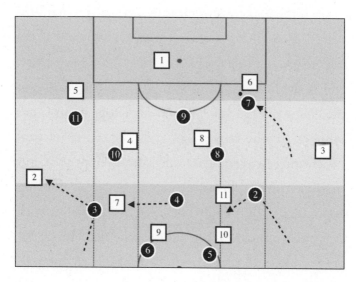

FOOTBALL IN A PANDEMIC

blocking passes into the opponent's narrow attackers, as well as covering the third-man pass out towards the advancing full-backs. City's full-backs (2, 3) positioned themselves higher, and narrower, now starting alongside the defensive midfielder (4), with the both centre-backs (5, 6) man for man against the opponent's two highest attackers.

City's full-backs (2, 3) covered the two attacking midfielders from their outside shoulders, as the defensive midfielder (4) zonally protected in between. Because the width in a 4-2-2-2 structure is provided by the full-backs, City maintained enough of a central presence to deal with direct play, while allowing instant pressing access into the wide areas, should the front line have forced a pass into the opponent's full-backs.

In a more aggressive pressing approach, Guardiola placed an additional central screener in front of the double pivot courtesy of City's own 4-2-3-1 structure, which the head coach used more than ever before in the Premier League in 2020/21. Therefore, it was City's number 10 who moved alongside the centre-forward (9), creating two central screeners. It was imperative this first line wasn't split with passes in between, allowing opponents to then easily break City's second line with quick play around. When either of the first line (9, 10) pressed forward, they forced the centre-back one way, while still covering access into their specific double-pivot opponent. Once play was forced over to the full-back, City's forward (9) took up a half -and-half role between the opponent's double pivot, and the closest centre-back.

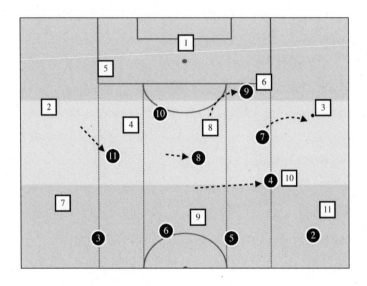

The narrow position of the closest winger (7) also blocked – either inside channel from centre-back to attacking midfielder, or even into an inside-moving winger. As the winger (7) then approached the ball, it was imperative they weren't beaten by a dribble back inside, continuing to force the full-back down the touchline.

Opponents using a 4-2-3-1 often pushed their attacking midfielder towards the wide area in reaction to this particular press, where City's closest defensive midfielder (4) aggressively followed man for man. The remaining defensive midfielder (8) and farthest winger (11) narrowed significantly in these moments, only leaving the opponent's farthest full-back unmarked.

It was important that the front line (9, 10) were organised, and their aggressive pressure individually well-timed. When pressing all the way on to the goalkeeper, the high attacker couldn't press and cover access into the double pivot, as well as the closest centre-back. Therefore, in these moments, City's defensive midfielder on the same side aggressively pushed on to the opponent's double pivot. The other defensive midfielder remained deeper, responsible for covering the opponent's attacking midfielder.

This aggressive pressure on to the goalkeeper often disrupted shorter build-up, forcing the play long, as opposed to regaining possession higher. From here, City had enough numbers to centrally screen the midfield, with a deeper five vs. four overload to compete for any longer passes.

An alternate method against the 4-2-3-1 specifically saw Guardiola use arguably his most aggressive pressing strategy of the season. When up against teams who almost exclusively built short via their double pivot, City formed a three-man back line for much longer periods, with the goalkeeper also much higher, covering the spaces in behind. As one of the central midfielders (8) joined the central forward (9) screen, the full-back (2) on the same side also started in a much higher position than in any pressing strategy seen under Guardiola.

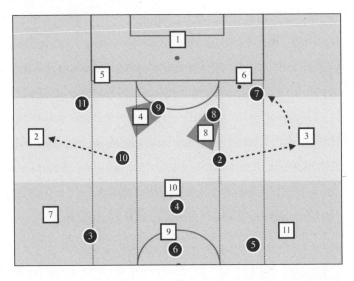

The opposition's 4-2-3-1 still meant City's defensive midfielder (4) had a permanent man to deal with, as Guardiola's wingers still required cover behind their inward press. This meant one full-back (2) covered one wide area, with the more conservative attacking midfielder (10) covering the opposite side. If the opposing attacking midfielder moved across to support around an aerial pass towards the full-back, then the defensive midfielder (4) once again followed.

But when up against two central forwards in a 4-4-2, City's central screen took over the highest pressing duties. The second line was predominantly composed of both wingers (7, 11) and the two defensive midfielders (4, 8), and their positioning was crucial. They covered the inside channel as a pair, prohibiting any play from the opposing centre-back into the inverted winger, or dropping central forward. But each of the two were also required to aggressively press their respective opponent when needed, continuing to force the ball away from the central lane.

Depending on how direct the opposition was from their 4-4-2, City's construction of the front line differed. Against less direct opponents, they continued to place the central forward (9) and highest attacking midfielder (10) in the first line of pressure. But against opponents

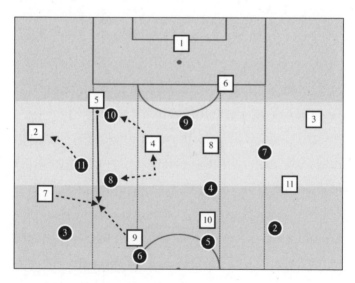

who played directly into the two centre-forwards, City's centre-backs required additional cover in front.

In order to place the defensive midfielder (4) deeper, City formed a front-line screen via the centre-forward, and the farthest winger. The closest winger then began much deeper, only pressing outwards towards the full-back when required. The two remaining central midfielders then covered the outside shoulders of the opponent's double pivot, with City's back line dealing with the front four.

The key to this strategy was the central forward continuously forcing the play towards the outside, giving more time for the farthest winger to narrow, and leaving the farthest opposing full-back free. But on the rare occasions where the opponents switched across to their temporarily free full-back – and didn't play directly into their central forward pairing – City's narrow winger recovered back, and pressed from behind.

8

Mid-Block

TEAMS WHO don't necessarily defend high up the pitch and close to their opponent's goal, nor deep within their own half, often utilise a mid-block strategy. Therefore, the main aim is to defend through the middle section of the pitch, stopping the opposition from playing through the block.

Naturally this involves all outfielders remaining compact and close together, and dropping into a defensive shape which doesn't engage too high, allowing the opponent to move forward with the ball. However, this is then merged with holding a line which still leaves some space in behind, where the goalkeeper can then act as a sweeper for direct play over the block. It's unrealistic to expect any team to press with intensity for the entire duration of a match, so this mid-block strategy is often used by teams who need to defend while preserving or regaining energy, before then increasing the defensive intensity once more. The mid-block is also used by teams as a primary defensive strategy, often focused around the central areas of the pitch, and stifling the opponent's creative central players. Defending from a mid-block can also encourage the opposition forward just enough, to then be exploited in behind their back line, particularly through incisive attacking transitions.

Dean Smith led Aston Villa back to the Premier League in 2019, before securing their survival on the final day of the 2019/20 season with a 1-1 draw away at West Ham. Staying up by just one point, Villa also failed to keep an away clean sheet all season, ending with a -26 goal difference.

Fast forward to 2020/21 and Villa's defensive displays significantly improved, keeping the third-most clean sheets in the entire division. They produced 20 blocks more than the league average through 2020/21 compared to 13 fewer than the average in 2019/20. Villa had a 12 per cent increase in the efficiency of their press, better recognising the moments when to engage the ball, and when to hold off within their block. This was split evenly through both higher pressing and deeper defending, as the entirety of the outfield block were much more organised, disciplined, and successful when engaging opponents in various areas of the pitch. Usually this stemmed from their compact mid-block in the moments prior to pushing up, or dropping back further.

Villa also ended the season with a +9 goal difference, some 35 better than the season prior. Their improved use of the mid-block soon benefited their overall attacking play, as after luring opponents forward, Villa frequently exploited the space in behind, registering the fifth-most counter-attacks across 2020/21, compared to the 14th most the year before.

4-4-2

Aston Villa utilised two distinct structures in attack, which naturally had an immediate effect on how they converted into a mid-block as they lost possession. The first of these came as the 4-2-3-1 reorganised into a 4-4-2 for prolonged defensive spells. In order to allow the full-backs and wingers to reposition from their respective attacking roles, Villa's central forward and number 10 quickly narrowed to form a tight pairing, limiting any central progression for the opposition. Should the opponents then target the wider spaces upon a regain, Villa's recovering wide players were working back anyway and would engage the play.

From Villa's 4-2-3-1 in attack, one of the two defensive midfielders always remained behind the ball, with the other moving forward on occasion. But because this particular forward run was usually in place of a higher team-mate – the number 10 for example – Villa could quickly reset their central midfield pairing, adding to their already strong central protection via the first line.

Once set into their 4-4-2 block, the central forward (9) and attacking midfielder (10) would alternatively press the opposing centre-backs, predominantly forcing the play outwards. As one moved forward (9), the other dropped and narrowed slightly (10), stopping a reverse pass back inside which would split the pair. The sole priority for this first-line pairing was not to be split by any central pass.

The speed at which they then pressed was also important as this pressure focused more on forcing the play towards the wide areas, as opposed to directly regaining the ball. However, the usual cues and triggers to increase the intensity of pressure such as slower, inaccurate, and/or bobbling passes, a poor first touch, or when the receiver was off balance, all still applied.

When this pressure didn't encourage the play wide, or the opposition were insistent on breaking through centrally, centre-backs would often switch the play between themselves. The safest way to do this was to turn back towards their own goal, keeping

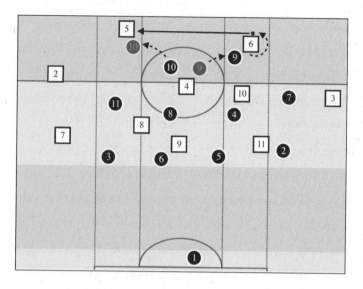

the ball on the safer side and well away from Villa's
first-line presser. After turning and playing across to
their centre-back team-mate, Villa's other attacker
(10) within their first line would press outwards, still
covering any central access. However, this safe-side
turn back before passing across took much longer than
simply moving the ball across the body, while still
facing Villa's front line. Therefore, Smith's block had
more than enough time to slide across, and prepare for
play moving towards the other side of the pitch. The
second and third lines especially benefited from this,
repositioning to deal with new opponents now closer
to the ball.

As Villa's next player pressed forward (10) they did
so at a fairly average pace, certainly not sprinting out

unless an interception was highly possibly. This almost delayed pressure as the ball moved across allowed Villa's original presser (9) enough time to drop back, and narrow. Otherwise a press out too quick wouldn't provide enough time for their high team-mate (9) to reposition, and block the central passes through. Plus, with Villa often remaining in their mid-block for considerable periods, maximising concentration and conserving energy were crucial to its success. Therefore, too rash and energetic individual pressing would have actually contributed to the strategy's downfall. So maintaining a reasonable speed during this jump out was very important, still putting the opposing centre-back under enough pressure to become slightly disrupted.

Smith's mid-block was especially effective when Villa as a whole remained patient and moved across with the ball as one entire outfield unit. By moving in time with these sideways passes, the opposition often grew frustrated by a lack of forward options, particularly through the central spaces. This resulted in the opposing back line searching for direct passes over Villa's first two lines, either playing into for flick ons and aerial duels, or on to for runs penetrating in behind.

Here, the goalkeeper's positioning was key, staying connected to the back line as they both stepped up, and dropped off. Emiliano Martínez often managed his positioning well, ready to engage any passes hit towards the spaces behind Villa's back four. With Tyrone Mings (72 per cent of aerial challenges won) and Ezri Konsa (69 per cent) as the first-choice centre-back pairing, Villa were also comfortable when dealing with any direct, aerial central passes played into opposing forwards, or late-running midfielders.

The management of distances between Villa's lines was also impressive, with Mings often leading the way from a vocal perspective. In the rare moments where Villa's front line failed to cover the central splitting pass, the depth from the second line, and in particular the central midfield pairing, covered these spaces, with the entire back line narrowing and stepping up when appropriate. With the central midfield duo often slightly deeper than their winger team-mates in Villa's second line anyway, they minimised the spaces between the lines for opposing attacking midfielders to receive in. This also helped to secure the second phase of any central passes, with anywhere up to four Villa players available to simultaneously condense on to the ball, and secure possession from within their defensive block.

When central play simply wasn't an option, the opposition soon focused on creating from the wide areas.

However, the opposing centre-backs would still try and instigate central play by stepping into midfield with the ball. Here, Villa's front line then increased their individual pressure, with a change of focus now attempting to regain the ball when the centre-backs became less connected, while still maintaining their central screening responsibilities via an outward curved press.

As the play began to move wider, Villa's closest first-line presser (9) began to change their angle of approach slightly, now covering the opponent's closest attacking midfielder. As a result, Villa's other player in their first line dropped even deeper, often marking the opposing pivot much closer than previous. From here, Villa's central midfield could begin to side across slightly earlier, often moving just before the ball was released

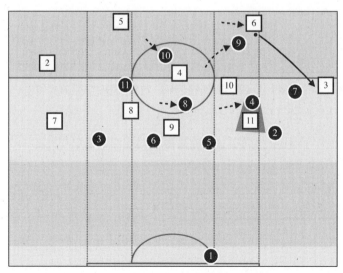

towards the wide area. If Villa's pressing attacker (9) didn't cover the pass through the inside channel as they approached the ball, then Villa's closest central midfielder (8) wouldn't have been able to move across and cover access into a narrow opposing winger, or widening central forward.

Villa's own winger (7) remained slightly ahead of the central midfield pair, ready to jump forward should the opposing centre-back advance past the first presser (9). This positioning also helped cut out any passes which could break past Villa's second line, with this slightly higher starting position often encouraging the opposing centre-back to play passes over.

Whenever Villa's wingers took up a more reserved position, then access into the opposing full-back was naturally much easier. However, this did encourage the full-back to begin deeper, where Villa continued to force the play along the touchline. Opposing wingers then made runs back towards the wide area, where Villa's full-back (2) closely followed to stop turns forward. As long as they weren't beaten in this one vs. one along the touchline, then Villa often locked the play into one wide area, with the opposition progressing forward slightly, but limited regarding their threat to Villa's goal from there.

Villa's first-line presser (9) would also work back slightly after their initial pressure to stop the opposing full-back from restarting the move, helping the closest central midfielder (8) screen and cover passes into the opposition's central midfield unit. The opposing centre-back would then have to drop considerably in order to initiate a switch across, which again cost significant time and energy. As this occurred, Villa's block then began to reset before moving across with the ball, once again staying connected to maintain their central compactness and forcing the opposition along the opposite wide area.

Villa's wider trap could also deal with the direct pass over their second line, now targeting either a very wide winger – thus skipping out the full-back – or into an overlapping full-back as the winger moved inside. From the 4-4-2 block, different Villa players pressed out to this pass, with the cover inside then crucial in stopping the second phase of this attacking move.

If the opposing full-back was particularly high, then Villa's own full-back (2) would jump out to meet the aerial pass into the wide area. Depending on the height and positioning of the inverted winger, Villa's secondary players (4, 7, 8) in this moment would adapt to cover the closest opponents. Naturally, as this aerial pass was challenging to control for the opposing full-back, flick ons, and early first-time passes proved key as they tried to secure the ball back inside of Villa's block.

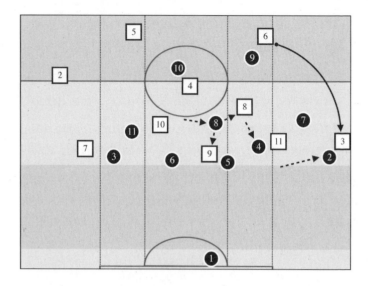

The closest central midfielder (8) would often cover inside of the full-back's (2) wide pressure, especially if the opposing winger was also supporting through the wide area.

Villa's other central midfielder (4) then moved across to support any secondary pressure, also able to add further pressure on the opposing centre-forward, or attacking midfielder, depending on where the ball was directed. The winger (7) would also screen inside, as well as pressing backwards touches from the opposing full-back. But with this particular pass often hit to encourage forward progress, the winger predominantly took up a screening role to stop passes back inside, aimed at the opposing attacking midfielder.

Alternately, the full-back stayed connected to their back line, often seen when up against a back three. Some opponents would also convert into a back three mid-game, adding an extra presence alongside their centre-backs via one of their defensive midfielders dropping. Both opposing full-backs then started slightly higher, with the wingers moving inside. Villa's front line then found it more difficult to stop opponents stepping into midfield, while still blocking any central access.

Therefore, Villa's entire block deepened, with the second line in particular now beginning closer to the back line of four, and slightly narrower than seen previous. This again encouraged the play wide, with the winger (7) mainly focusing on covering the inside channel. However, they would still position themselves in such a position to allow for wider interceptions, which often meant the opposing full-back had to take up a position right against the touchline, to create a more secure passing option around.

The narrower position of the central midfield pair (4, 8) accounted for the change in opposition structure, and occupation of Villa's entire back line. Here, they prioritised the spaces around their centre-back team-mates, while also adding numbers to the cover of passes back inside.

It was very common to see teams attempt to work the ball into a central position via a first-time pass back inside from the wide area. Sometimes it's possible to take advantage of the eagerness shown by some pressing players, who choose to aggressively move towards a free player receiving in the wide area. However, this first-time pass negates any oncoming pressure, as the ball is released well before the pressure arrives on to the opponent. And as the defender has now jumped out of the central spaces, there is just enough space vacated to receive a pass back inside, and attack from within a block.

So Villa accounted for this by not placing the immediate pressure on to the opposing full-back, instead allowing them to move forward upon receiving,

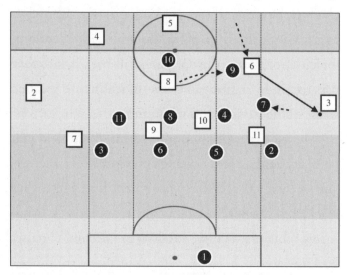

while Villa quickly rearranged before eventually dealing with the advancing wide player.

As the ball travelled out to the full-back, Villa's back line began to drop, with the second line moving over towards the ball. Once either the winger (7) or closest central midfielder (8) had dropped alongside the inside shoulder of their full-back (2) team-mate, and in a position to cover narrow forward runs, and the passes back inside, Villa's full-back (2) then pressed out towards the ball.

Although this allowed the opposition to progress further forward than previous, and possibly gain some attacking momentum – depending on the state of the match – this strategy and defensive movement accounted for play sent along the touchline, as well as back inside into central opponents. Some teams then focused on switching full-back to full-back, accounting for Villa's narrower second line. Yet with the distance of pass relatively large, and the level of technical execution required high, Villa were comfortable at sliding across, and then, if needed, setting up a quick low block to deal with play on the other side of the pitch.

4-1-4-1

The second attacking structure Smith selected through 2020/21 was a 4-3-3. In relation to the mid-block strategy, this placed one fewer player within Villa's first line but gave them extra security in the spaces between the lines. Compared to the use of a 4-4-2, for the most part, the 4-1-4-1 mid-block was set up slightly deeper, with the attacking focus then geared more towards transitional moments, especially through the wide areas, and Villa's two wingers.

With the central forward (9) now alone in the first line, opposing centre-backs stepped forward with the ball more as Smith often selected this structure when facing a double pivot. Here, it was essential that central access was still screened, with the centre-forward (9) prioritising blocking the closest opposing midfielder to the ball. This screening, before eventually applying pressure to disrupt the oncoming centre-back, allowed Villa's second line to reset, and prepare for a wider pressing trap.

It was important that the centre-forward encouraged the driving forward towards the wide area, often prohibiting the centre-back from switching back across, unless they turned safe side. In these moments, Villa's far winger (7) would jump forward and press inwards, especially when a pass particularly presented itself to be pressed.

But as the centre-forward (9) then began their outward press, Villa's two central midfielders (8,

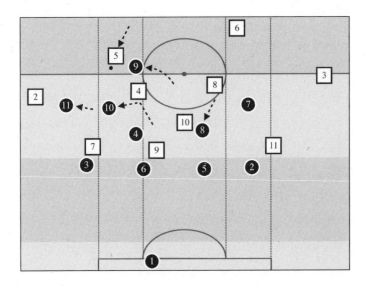

10) initially moved to tightly mark the opposition's double pivot. The closest of the two (10) would cover the outside shoulder, with the farthest (8) marking on the inside, ready for disguised, or reversed passes back inside. As the central forward (9) then moved closer, they could cut off the angles into the opposition's double pivot. This would then free Villa's central midfield (8, 10) to move across with the ball, and block passing lanes, as opposed to solely man marking an opponent.

Villa's closest central midfielder (10), for example, could now cover access through the inside channel, blocking a narrow winger. In turn, this enabled Villa's closest winger (11) to position themselves wider, limiting the passing options around the outside of Villa's second line. The defensive midfielder (4) then moved across with the ball, predominantly screening ahead of the opposition's centre-forward. These movements across the pitch were again only really enabled as Villa's farthest central midfielder (8) dropped to support ahead of the central defence, who's original opponent was still blocked by the centre-forward's (9) curving pressure.

Some opponents who used a double pivot also selected a back three, with the wing-backs providing the main elements of attacking width. Naturally, due to the central compactness of Villa's 4-1-4-1 mid-block, direct switches from wide centre-back to far wing-back proved enticing for opponents, especially as the centre-backs could still step forward with relative ease.

In these moments, Villa's central forward (9) again screened central access, blocking the closest defensive midfielder where possible. But with the opposition now having three centre-backs spread across the pitch, Villa's central forward (9) only aggressively engaged when the middle centre-back attempted to drive forward through the central lane. By design, the opposition naturally built with an initial focus through the inside channel, attempting to find their two inside-forwards.

But as the wide centre-back stepped forward, at some point Villa had to engage. It was often the

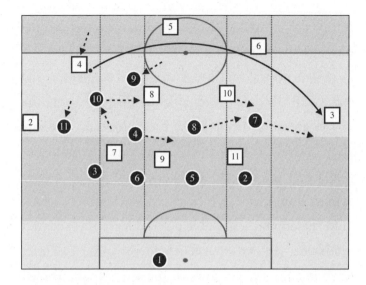

closest central midfielder (10) who approached the ball, ensuring they screened the opponent's inside-forward in the process. Villa's closest winger (11) would then deepen slightly, accounting for the higher average position of the opposing wing-back, now no longer a full-back moving forward. Villa's second line started very narrow once more, covering the opposing front line, and, if needed, enabling a central jump on to the opposition's double pivot.

Any switch across towards the opposite wide area predominantly saw the winger (7) apply the first element of pressure, with the full-back (2) often more reserved compared to Villa's 4-4-2 mid-block. As the ball travelled, the winger (7) recovered diagonally to cover any aggressive first touch from the receiving wing-back, as well as encouraging the play to continue through the wide area.

Villa's central midfield then moved across with the ball, with the defensive midfielder (4) prioritising the spaces ahead of the opposing centre-forward, and any early passes hit back inside. The central midfielder (8) closest towards the switch covered inside of their winger team-mate (7), focusing on blocking access back into the opponent's double pivot. The farthest central midfielder (10), now possibly higher than the ball after their initial jump out towards the centre-back, covered back across the pitch, again prohibiting passes back into the central lane.

There were some moments where the full-back (2) did jump forward, though, especially as the opposing winger dropped to support play through the wide area.

Against a more reserved full-back opponent, the winger (7) continued to press outwards, encouraging play to progress along the touchline. If they could also cut off a pass back inside into the opponent's closest defensive midfielder, then Villa's central midfielder (8) could cover a diagonal pass inside, as the opposing full-back frequently searched for the feet of the central forward where possible, especially when the winger dropped short.

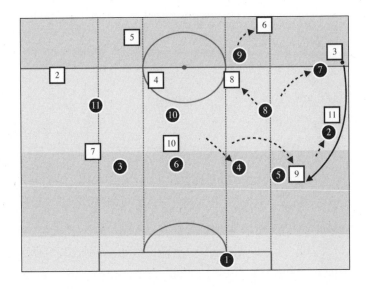

If Villa's pressing winger (7) performed a quicker, more direct press out, they covered more of the inside channel. The responsibility then fell on the closest central midfielder (8) to press on to the opponent's double pivot. The centre-forward (9) could also press from the other side of the ball in these moments, with the rest of the second line (10, 11) narrowing to block the central lane, especially whenever the defensive midfielder (4) began their cover into the back line.

The full-back (2) then pushed out to prohibit the winger from turning from any subsequent line pass, with the opposing central forward often forced to make bending runs into the wide area. Villa's own centre-forward (9) then moved across towards the ball, blocking switches on the ground to the opposition's far centre-back, while also in a position to press either the closest defensive midfielder, or centre-back. This positioning was also crucial to prohibit first-time passes played around the corner, which can be a particularly effective strategy against a full-back who has followed a dropping winger, as well as being a pass capable of matching a centre-forward's bending run beyond.

With Villa's back line now expanded, and very briefly exposed, they needed temporary cover and readjustments. The defensive midfielder (4) often filled in between the two centre-backs, especially as the closest (5) tracked the centre-forward's run into the wide area. Villa's remaining defenders (3, 6) then covered their respective opponents, ready to deal with early crosses, should the opposing centre-forward manage to connect with the pass in behind.

Another example of defensive midfield (4) coverage came as Villa's central forward (9) began with their slightly more aggressive press on to the middle centre-back, still forcing the play one way. The winger (7) then moved forward, again encouraging the play to be built around the outside of Villa's second line.

To further encourage this wider play, both of Villa's central midfielders (8, 10) then jumped on to the opposing double pivot, aggressively marking to place them under constant pressure. Just before the wing-back received the pass, the winger (7) covered access to the inside channel as they moved across.

Initially, Villa would try and leave the closest inside-forward unattached, so the wing-back, prior to receiving the sideways pass, would scan to look ahead, and see their team-mate unmarked. But as the ball was released wide from the centre-back, Villa's defensive midfielder (4) burst across, as the closest full-back (2) also jumped to stop a turn forward. This helped overload and create a two vs. one, with the winger (7) able to press and cover backwards passes if needed.

With both of Villa's central midfielders then closer to the ball than their direct opponent, they could screen

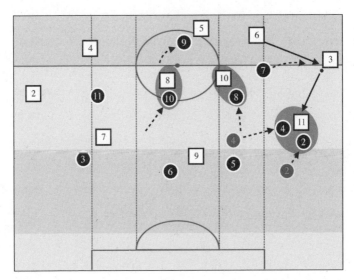

sets aimed back towards the centre. Pressure on to the inside-forward from both sides also prohibited any dribbling progress, as Villa demonstrated arguably their most aggressive pressing approach from their mid-block strategy.

The timing of this particular jump was naturally extremely important. Press too early, and the opposing wing-back would have turned back to switch the play along the central defence. Press too late, and the inside-forward could receive freely, face forwards, and combine with the rest of the narrow front line, targeting the central spaces now made bigger by Villa's aggressively pressing central midfield pair.

Although this strategy was used much less when compared to the others, it did help Villa manage momentum in some matches, certainly more so than any other pressing strategies or wider traps used via their mid-block defending.

9

Low Block

THE LOW block defensive strategy involves a side placing their entire team in an extremely deep position. The main rationale is simply to increase the difficulty for the opposition to create chances. By placing the back line deep inside the defensive half of the pitch, space in front of the goalkeeper can be particularly difficult to access.

By remaining compact from the first line to the last line of defence, spaces within the actual block itself, commonly referred to as 'between the lines', are also kept to a minimum. This makes it difficult for opponents to receive within the overall block, as aggressive defending can be instantly established on the ball carrier. Keeping compact from left to right then helps to stop any passes through the block, further troubling the opposition.

For the most part, play is then encouraged towards the wide areas as some spaces have to be conceded, no matter the defensive strategy, with the central areas often prioritised. But once the ball is wide, stopping diagonal passes over and crosses into the penalty area is key, not force the opponents away from the centre, but requiring them to find an alternative method to enter the penalty area from a different angle. On occasions play may be shown inside and forced towards the defensive traffic, particularly when the defending team has a numerical overload in the central areas. But for the most part, it's common to force the play outside.

As the lower block naturally requires lengthy periods of defending, and thus lots of time without entering the opponent's half, the reduced moments of attack are vital. If a team can maintain, or even enhance, their attacking effectiveness, as Leicester City did in 2015/16, then coupled with an organised and resolute low block, teams can beat just about anyone on their day.

Yet nearly all teams will adopt a low block at some point in a game, even if it's a temporary fix to deal with an an opponent's increase of attacking momentum. However, some sides will elect to prioritise this deeper defending and use it as their primary defensive strategy across a season, often accompanied by quick counter-attacking play.

To provide further defensive support and assistance, some teams will also add an extra player into the back line. Mauricio Pochettino would look to do this with Tottenham Hotspur, often building with a back four, to then defend with a back five. However, this wasn't always coupled with a deep low block.

José Mourinho took over at Tottenham from Pochettino in November 2019, and would adopt both a back four, and a back five across his tenure. However, there were moments when Mourinho went one further, using a defensive strategy which can be traced back to his time at Manchester United.

The Back Six – Manchester United

Three-time Premier League winner Mourinho, on occasion, added two extra players into the back line, taking an extremely guarded approach to repel key opposing threats. With United specifically, it was the wingers who recovered outside of the full-backs, from both a 4-3-3 and a 4-4-2 attacking structure. This established a plus-one overload in the back line as most teams converted into a front line of five when up against a lower block. Mourinho assigned this particular recovering role to those who'd had extensive experience as both a winger, and a full-back across their career. Ashley Young and Antonio Valencia stood out in this regard.

Opposing full-backs would only move forward to create a front five once the wingers had narrowed though. So United's initial full-backs (2, 3) then tracked these inward movements, essentially becoming a third and fourth centre-back during prolonged spells without the ball. Players such as Daley Blind, and Phil Jones, who had exposure at both full-back and centre-back, proved invaluable for this particular role.

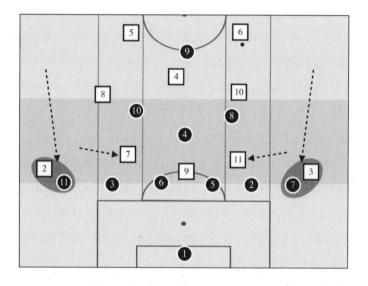

From United's 4-3-3, the central midfield trio (4, 8, 10) held their original positioning, screening the opposition's central threats placed in front of United's back line. Opponents were often forced to create around the block, where resulting crosses were straightforward to deal with via the condensed back line of six.

United's second line also kept an appropriate distance away from the defence as it was crucial that both units moved in tandem, dropping back as one and, when possible, squeezing forward together. This ensured spaces between the lines were kept to a minimum, while defending as deep as needed to minimise any threats in behind. But the back line were also positioned high enough to allow the midfield to press and block shots from range, particularly through the inside channels.

The opposition's attacking midfielders often moved into the wide areas purely out of frustration, as United's attacking midfielders (8, 10) then individually pressed outwards. This locked the play away from the centre while still blocking access into the narrow front line. This pressure also nullified cross-field passes targeting over United's back line, usually directed towards the farthest full-back, or winger. The trigger of a bigger touch instigated this wider pressure, primarily to stop the cross-field pass.

But this increase in defensive solidity came at the expense of a reduced counter-attacking threat. After a regain, United's second line (4, 8, 10) tried to connect into the central forward (9) as efficiently as possible. But even if the highest attacker was outstanding when running in behind, it was difficult to create chances on goal from the severe underload, and the considerable

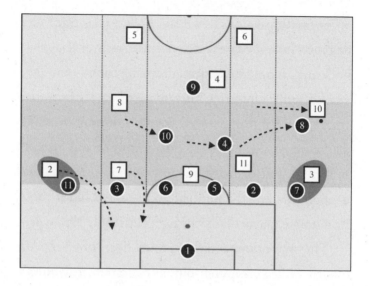

distance still required to reach the final third, let alone the goal itself.

The two widest midfielders (8, 10) also failed to replicate the secondary support which the wingers (7, 11) could have provided on the break. And thus with virtually no threat into the wide areas, the opposition pushed their full-backs as high as they needed, with minimal repercussions.

When up against a back-three system, Mourinho used a slightly different starting shape prior to the conversion into the back six. Opposing wing-backs were often positioned higher than full-backs in a back four, with a front trio already narrow, unlike the 4-3-3 Mourinho faced previously. So the 4-4-2 was then selected, as United's wingers started deeper than when used in the 4-3-3, creating a quicker recovery around the outside of their full-backs.

But as a caveat to this quicker transition, United's second line was now only made up of two midfielders (4, 8), resulting in less effective central blocking of the opponent's front line. Although this did add an extra player to the first line, the opponent's use of three central defenders still held an overload, easily addressing any counter-attacking play.

This change to a 2-2 ahead of the back six eventually caused United's multiple low-block issues, which would remain for Mourinho into 2020/21 with Tottenham Hotspur. The opposing back line of three soon spread wider, and because of the initial screening ahead of the double pivot, it became very difficult for United's first line (9, 10) to get across, and stop them dribbling into midfield. Although the first line (9) forced the play outside, either a quick turn back towards the middle centre-back, and a subsequent central pass through, or, a diagonal pass back inside from the advancing centre-back into their front line, regularly penetrated United's 6-2-2 low block.

From this second method, the opposing centre-backs predominantly passed into the central forward, or the farthest inside-forward. To free these two passing options, the farthest wing-back made decoy

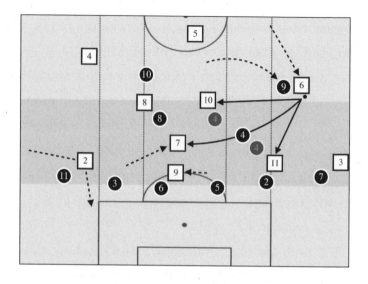

runs inside of United's deep winger (11), threatening to run blindside of the narrow full-back (3). This allowed the opponent's inside-forward to move into the central lane unattached, and receive a pass from the advancing centre-back. The central forward also moved on to United's farthest centre-back (6), stopping them from stepping out of the back line to cover the central spaces.

Although United's closest central midfielder (4) soon moved across to stop this pass back inside, they had to stop covering either the closest inside-forward, or the closest defensive midfielder in the process. So no matter where or how the closest central midfielder (4) pressed out towards the advancing wide centre-backs, a pass inside was always available.

The role of United's second-line pairing was then made even more difficult as they became responsible for pressing tighter on to the opposing double pivot. To block the wide centre-back advances, the first line widened. But with the second line further away from the back line, a simple splitting pass from the middle centre-back went all the way through to the opponent's front line, again breaking through Mourinho's low block.

The Back Six – Tottenham Hotspur

After his move to Tottenham, Mourinho attempted to revitalise the back-six, low block. His side quickly changed shape after losing possession via those players who were required to cover as little ground as possible. Physiologically this helped reduce the amount of additional work placed on these specific players. But from a tactical perspective, the quicker, and more fluid the conversion, the stronger the shift into the low-block strategy.

Through 2020/21 specifically, Mourinho tweaked those recovering players to deal with an emerging attacking strategy, particularly prevalent against the low block. Although opponents have continued to form a front line of five since Mourinho's departure from United, wingers holding the width more as the widest of the front five are often supported inside by two very high attacking midfielders. The 3-2-5 attacking shape has remained though, albeit with the full-backs now part of either the first or second line instead of overlapping forward.

The best example of how well Mourinho's latest version of the back-six, low-block strategy worked was ironically when he elected not to use it. When visiting the Etihad Stadium in February 2021, Tottenham deployed a 4-4-2 low block instead, comfortably losing the game 3-0. Manchester City's wingers often held incredibly wide positions, often luring Tottenham's full-backs away from their closest centre-back. The issue here with the back four is that no matter the positioning of the full-back, the attacking side has a method of breaking in behind.

Whenever Tottenham's full-back (3) tightly marked the wide winger, the gap between them and their closest centre-back (6) increased further, easily exploitable via a through pass. The winger, already in a forward-facing position, then moved from static and motionless, to maximum sprint speed with relative ease. Whereas Tottenham's full-back, who was at best side on, was already at a disadvantage, having to turn, before then sprinting back. If the winger held the width, receiving the ball to feet, underlapping runs from the attacking midfielder then exploited behind Tottenham's pressing full-back.

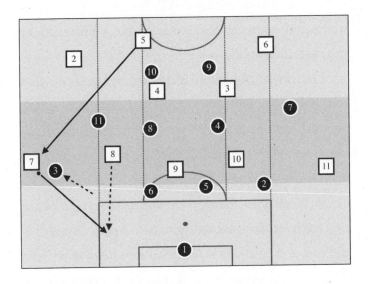

Alternatively, the full-back (3) remained within the inside channel, stopping the penetrative pass into the winger, or the run in behind from the attacking midfielder. But this meant far less pressure on to the receiving winger, who then repeatedly drove at Tottenham's back line.

If you stop the winger, the midfielder breaks through. If you stop the midfielder, the winger breaks through. A direct pass from centre-back to winger is also key here, allowing the attacking midfielder to push beyond.

A half-and-half position between the two was the full-back's (3) best option in this scenario. But as the low block already sacrificed a significant amount of territory, disguised play either around or through, as well as individual brilliance one vs. one, will eventually expose the full-back.

This is why Mourinho identified not only the need for a back six, but also an updated version to quash arguably the most effective route of breaking through a low block, without totally sacrificing any form of threat during counter-attacking moments.

So Mourinho changed the the initial shape before the back-six conversion into a 4-2-3-1, instead of the 4-4-2 or 4-3-3 seen previously with Manchester United. The responsibility of tracking the runs into the opponent's front five now fell on Tottenham's defensive midfielders (4, 8). The back six then formed as these players filled inside of their full-back (2, 3) team-mates, as opposed to the previously used wingers dropping around the outside for United.

But this required players capable of defending for long periods within the back line, while handling the increase of physical attributes required when defending in this area of the pitch. Mourinho's back six still faced aerial passes targeted towards the outer shoulders of the original two central defenders (5, 6). So for Tottenham specifically through 2020/21, Pierre-Emile Højbjerg proved the perfect dropping asset in this regard, with a 66 per cent aerial duel success rate, and comfortably the most ball recoveries for the team across the season.

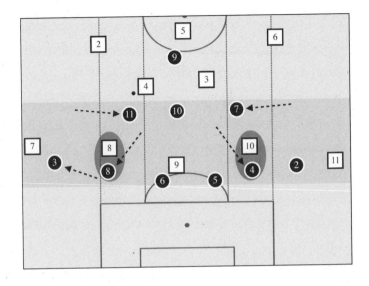

Tottenham's second line (7, 10, 11) held their original positions, blocking access into the opponent's three narrow attackers, while also funnelling the ball into the wide areas, limiting those inside-channel penetrations.

Tottenham's defensive midfielders (4, 8), now positioned inside the back line, allowed the full-backs (2, 3) to press into wide areas when needed. As play was continuously forced into the opposing wingers, Tottenham's block was strengthened with their full-backs much stronger when defending the wide areas, compared to the wingers recovering back as seen with United.

Nevertheless, some full-backs can still be exposed when defending one vs. one, particularly those who are better suited to a wing-back role, where their wider defending is covered by an extra central defender from the back three. Chelsea's Marcos Alonso, a particularly talented wing-back, is a prime example of this, often unable to defend the wide areas when deployed as a left-back in a back four. Similar arguments can be made around Spurs' Serge Aurier, and Matt Doherty. With this in mind, Tottenham's covering defensive midfielder (8) proved invaluable defensive support, especially when positioned deeper than their full-back team-mate.

In an attempt to enhance movements in behind, and remain onside, some wingers will also start slightly withdrawn, as opposed to right on the edge of the offside line. Although this positioning can pull the full-back (3) out even further away from the closest defender (6), Tottenham's defensive midfield (4, 8) cover nullified both of these particular advantages, protecting down the line if the full-back (3) was beaten by a dribble around the outside, or via a through ball.

Another benefit of any back six is the wide defending performed by the two closest defenders (now 3 and 8), which means a back four remains intact to defend the width of the penalty area. In the extremely rare moments when the opposing winger beat both of the first two defenders (3 and 8), Tottenham still overloaded the opposing runners into their penalty area, quite often in a four vs. two. The closest centre-back (6) to the play would predominantly cover the front-post area, prohibiting low crosses in front of Tottenham's goal – a particularly common attacking strategy from wingers who drive around the outside. Mourinho's side then had enough players to cover both cut-back deliveries towards the edge of the penalty area, and efforts chipped towards runners at the far post.

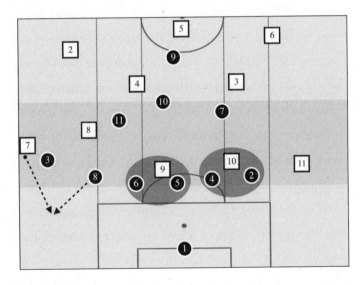

Crucially, though, maintaining a 6-3-1 structure also benefited Tottenham's counter-attacking play, as all three of their attacking midfielders (7, 10, 11) now filled the second line, as opposed to the more defensive players utilised within United's second line. This created a much stronger threat after a regain, as the players now carrying the ball forward were among Tottenham's best attackers.

Harry Kane dropping deeper as the central forward (9) further added to Tottenham's transitional play, particularly adept when protecting the ball, providing extra seconds for the attacking midfield trio to reposition if needed. Kane's movements away from the opposition's centre-backs also made him more difficult to mark in the first instance, giving Tottenham's back six a better chance of finding the centre-forward from the first pass out. Tanguy Ndombele's ability as the central attacking midfielder (10) to receive and manage the ball underloaded also proved invaluable as Tottenham's breakaways from their back-six, low block carried a much stronger threat than those seen by United under Mourinho.

However, Spurs' increased counter-attacking threat was hampered slightly when opponents had three players in their first line, either through a permanent back three or through some form of conversion. When opposing full-backs joined the front line in a 2-3-5 shape, teams had just two defenders within the first two lines of build-up.

When the wing-backs moved high from the 3-4-3 structure, opponents had three defenders in the first two lines. But with the most modern conversion occurring through the attacking midfielders, opponents now had all four defenders within the first two lines. Therefore, although Mourinho's latest back-six idea was an improvement in both defence and counter-attack, the updated opposing 3-2-5 shape saw a much stronger defensive base from the opposition, ready to deal with Tottenham's counter-attacking play.

After some initial success, opponents soon began to vary their attacking approach against Mourinho's latest strategy, further altering the players who formed the front five. It was now no longer the case that either both full-backs or both attacking midfielders moved forward simultaneously. Instead, attacking strategies through 2020/21 have shown more variety than ever in the attacking phase, with one winger inverting to allow a full-back overlap, as the other winger maintains the width, for example.

The first issue to present itself came as Tottenham's full-back (3) followed an inverting winger too tightly, mistiming passing them on to the closest defensive midfielder (8), briefly allowing the opposing full-back to receive and move in behind. But as more concerning errors soon emerged, the secondary cover provided by the defensive midfielders (4, 8), and central defensive (5, 6) presence eventually helped deal with the next phase of this particular attack.

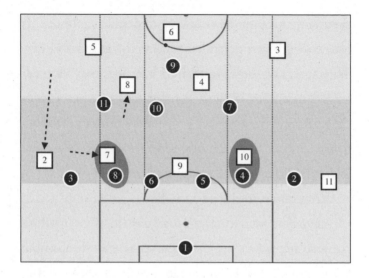

As Tottenham's adapted 6-3-1 maintained its compactness, and effectiveness, while still best positioning their four most attacking players to counter-attack themselves, opposing sides then tried a more aggressive attacking strategy, particularly when beginning with a back four.

Once the front line of five was established through high attacking midfielders, opponents began to push both full-backs forward in support. This particular attacking strategy mirrored that of Sheffield United through 2019/20, albeit through a different player performing the actual overlap.

Despite opponents now leaving just two centre-backs and a single pivot against Tottenham's counter-attacking play, the forward-running full-backs eventually dragged Mourinho's wider midfielders (7, 11) into much deeper positions, forced to work back to stop opponents creating a wide overload. Tottenham's wider midfielders (7, 11) were then unable to take advantage of the extremely attractive spaces left by the overlapping full-back, as Tottenham's central attacking midfielder (10) also dropped back to maintain the screen in front of the opposing centre-forward.

Tottenham's own central forward (9) then took over the goalside positioning behind the single pivot, as the wingers (7, 11) could no longer assist in covering central passes due to increasing defensive responsibilities. From the opposition's perspective, it predominantly reduced Tottenham's counter-attacking abilities, as any resulting crossing play was comfortably dealt with by the sheer volume of players now defending deep for Tottenham. Despite the best attacking intentions from the opposition as they committed these extra players forward, they actually compacted Tottenham's block further, which proved even more difficult to break down in the long run.

As Tottenham grew accustomed to this assertive attacking strategy, they also managed to improve when passing on opponents who rotated inside. Initially, Tottenham's wide attacking midfielder (11) simply followed the overlapping full-back, with the defensive

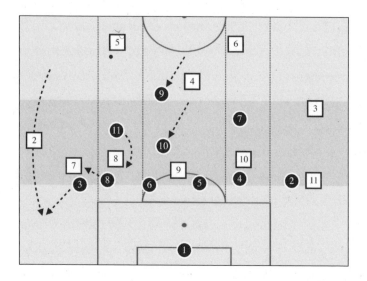

midfielder (8) and full-back (3) covering their original opponent. But to keep the wide attacking midfielder (11) more central for counter-attacks, the full-back (3) pressed out toward the overlap, as the defensive midfielder (8) quickly followed before changing opponents.

Tottenham's wide attacking midfielder (11), although much deeper than they would have liked, was at least now better positioned to break forward through the inside channel, and eventually around the opposing centre-backs if possible. Despite successfully adapting to opposing changes here, the back-six, low block was eventually broken down via a particular attacking strategy which also troubled Mourinho with United.

When up against a 3-4-3, the high wing-backs created the front line of five once more, with Tottenham still deploying their defensive midfielders into the back line. Just as with United though, Tottenham then moved to a 2-2 structure ahead of the back six, and wider centre-back dribbles into midfield quickly resurfaced. While the initial response was again to widen the first line, in doing so they could no longer screen in front of the opponent's central midfield. Tottenham's second line were then forced away from the back six, now tightly man marking on to the double pivot, to stop them turning and playing forward so easily.

Although this stopped progress via the centre-backs stepping in, a simple pass from the middle centre-back again penetrated straight into the central spaces instead, especially when the opposing central midfielders widened to create this bigger central space to pass through. Frequent bounce passes between the opponent's middle centre-back and double pivot also pulled Tottenham's second line higher than they wanted, further increasing the space for the opposing front trio to receive in.

Whenever one of Tottenham's second line backed off to block this splitting pass through, the corresponding central midfielder was able to receive and turn unmarked, and play into the opponent's front line. With this central pass now threatening, Tottenham's front line were constantly moving back and forth between narrow and wider starting positions, as the opposition had answers to Tottenham's changes. If only one of Tottenham's front line widened, then the wider centre-back would simply step forward with the ball through the other inside channel, or continue to play penetrative passes through the central spaces.

Mourinho also faced a 3-4-3 without a fixed central forward, with opponents deploying a much more fluid forward trio who no longer needed wider decoy runs from the farthest wing-back to help them receive passes. When Tottenham had two players (9, 10) in their first line the opponent's widest forwards dragged Tottenham's defensive midfielders (4, 8) into the back line much earlier. This enabled the central member of the trio to drop and receive, taking further advantage of the enlarged gap behind Tottenham's second line.

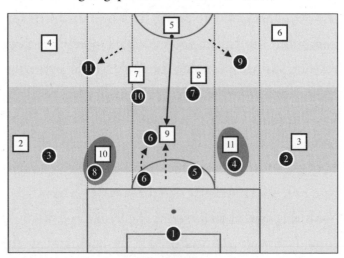

When Tottenham's centre-backs (5, 6) held their ground, and didn't engage with the dropping forward, they blocked any potential pass in behind, predominantly aimed through the inside channels. However, this meant the central attacker could receive and turn freely, well within Tottenham's low block. Yet when Tottenham's centre-back (6) did press out of the back line, although prohibiting a free turn to face the goal, it also created exploitable gaps for the opposition to penetrate through, especially via third-man runs.

There were also moments when the fluid front trio positioned themselves through the same inside channel, and Tottenham's defensive midfielders (4, 8) then struggled to understand how best to preserve the back line, while also dealing with the threats between the lines. This particular attacking strategy came after Tottenham's first line (9, 10) had narrowed once more, with the wider centre-backs again stepping into midfield. Even though Tottenham's first line tried to apply pressure on to these advances, the opposition's forwards were already positioned ready to receive a pass on the same side as the ball.

Further to receiving passes straight from the wide centre-back, the opposing front line also made runs back into the central lane, just as the wider centre-back was running out of space to drive into. The middle of the three forwards would then occupy Tottenham's closest central defender (6), stopping them from stepping into the central areas on the resulting pass back inside.

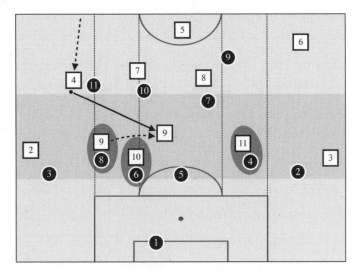

Both of Tottenham's defensive midfielders (4, 8) were still attached to the widest of the opposing trio, but the well-timed movements back into the centre were difficult to track, particularly for Tottenham's closest defensive midfielder (8).

The opposition had thus found another method to access their front line, penetrating through Mourinho's updated back-six, low-block idea. And until Tottenham placed three within their second line, enabling better cover against central access into the front line and dealing with wider centre-back advances, Tottenham's defensive struggles continued. Mourinho didn't last the season.

The Back Six – Everton

Mourinho wasn't the only manager to have their back-six, low block exploited in 2020/21, as Carlo Ancelotti also attempted a similar defensive strategy, predominantly to solve those same attacking problems created through the inside channels. Everton selected an almost identical strategy with the 6-2-2, but instead of tight marking on to the opponent's converted double pivot – as the full-back moved inside, now alongside the defensive midfielder – they instead placed their sole focus on the two attacking midfielders, following every single one of their runs and movements, no matter the speed or direction.

Although Everton faced a converted 4-3-3, the opposition still formed a similar attacking shape to the 3-4-3 which Mourinho struggled with. However, the opposing attacking midfielders quickly recognised that they had a permanent shadow throughout the game, and soon adapted their positioning. The pair stopped moving so high, and instead of breaking into the front line they left the central spaces all together, now moving into a much wider position. As Everton's defensive midfielders (4, 8) aggressively followed these movements, new issues arose against this particular back-six, low-block idea.

The positioning of Everton's wider midfielders (7, 11) often stopped the wider centre-backs from stepping into midfield, a core issue Mourinho's strategy struggled with. But persistent shorter passes between the opponent's first two lines pulled Everton's first line (9, 10) much higher, once again creating relatively simple access into the huge central space, and a dropping centre-forward (9). This space was enhanced further by the opponent's attacking midfielders' continued wider movements.

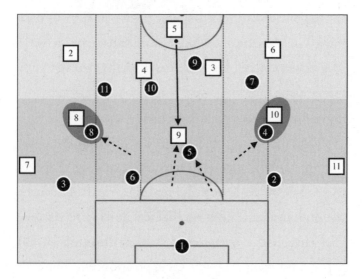

To disrupt the middle centre-back's penetrative forward passing, one of Everton's first line (9) then jumped forward to press much earlier. But the central spaces were still vacated, as the defensive midfielders (8, 10) were continuously pinned by the wide-moving attacking midfielders.

So play continued into the opposing central forward, albeit now much earlier due to Everton's increased pressure via their first line. But the opposing double pivot left free by Everton's highest presser (9), now moved to either receive directly from the middle centre-back, or from a set-back via the central forward.

The more reserved of Everton's front line (10) often did well to stop the third-man pass between the opponent's two double pivots, though, by covering the inside shoulder of their direct opponent. But ultimately there were still too many combinations available to penetrate into the central areas, easily accessing the space just in front of Everton's central defence.

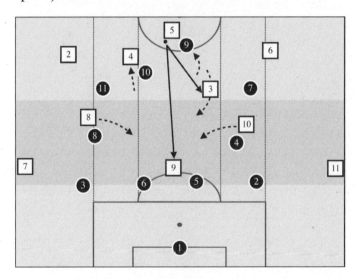

A staggered double pivot from the opposition then proved extremely efficient in breaking Everton's attempted back-six, low-block strategy. With one of the opponents moving closer to their own back line, the other moved forward, often as the player left free by Everton's more committed pressing player (9).

After the pass had moved through Everton's initial pressure on to the ball, the opposing attacking midfielders would also move back inside, further supporting the central play into the highest forward, creating multiple incisive combinations to regularly attack Everton's central defence. This was the exact opposite of what a low block is designed to do.

Bibliography

[1] – Dupont G, Nedelec M, McCall A, McCormack D, Berthoin S, Wisløff U. Effect of 2 soccer matches in a week on physical performance and injury rate. Am J Sports Med 2010; 38:1752-1758.

[2] – Ekstrand J, Waldén M, Hägglund M. A congested football calendar and the wellbeing of players: correlation between match exposure of European footballers before the World Cup 2002 and their injuries and performances during that World Cup. Br J Sports Med 2004; 38:493-497.

[3] – Bengtsson H, Ekstrand J, Hägglund M. Muscle injury rates in professional football increase with fixture congestion: an 11-year follow-up of the UEFA Champions League injury study. Br J Sports Med 2013; 47:743-747.

[4] – Waters A, Lovell G. An examination of the home field advantage in a professional English soccer team from a psychological standpoint. Football Studies. 2002; 5(1): 46- 59.

[5] – Reade J, Schreyer D, Singleton C. 2020. Echoes: what happens when football is played behind closed doors?

[6] – Dohmen T, Sauermann, J. 2016. 'Referee Bias'. *Journal of Economic Surveys*, 30(4): 679–695.

[7] – Wolfson S, Wakelin D, Lewis M. 2005. 'Football supporters' perceptions of their role in the home advantage'. *Journal of Sports Sciences*, 23(4): 365–374.

[8] – Sors F, Grassi M, Agostini T, Murgia M. The sound of silence in association football: Home advantage and referee bias decrease in matches played without spectators. Eur J Sport Sci. 2020 Nov 29:1-9.

Websites
BBC Sport
ESPN
The Guardian
InStat
Premier Injuries
The Premier League
Sky Sports
The Telegraph
Wyscout